五季味津

Five Seasons in the Kitchen

Zen Inspired Vegan Cooking

Avital Sebbag

TO SEE THE BEAUTY OF THE UNIVERSE
BETWEEN EARTH AND SKY.
A BUD APPEARS
AFTER THE RAIN
CONTAINS THE ESSENCE OF LIFE
SO PURE AND FRESH
SEASONS GO
SEASONS COME.
AVITAL SEBBAG

For my parents, Gabriel (of Blessed Memory)
and Simcha Sebbag who gave me life.
For my sons Yossi, Mikey, Gabriel (Babi),
Joey and Jonathan.

五季味津

Photography

Michal Lenart

Hebrew Editor

Tamar Mor-Sela

English Translation

Elizabeth Zauderer

Art and Design

Eddie Goldfine

Consultants

Efrat Marciano

Orit Rachmani

Styling

Ingrid Kutner

Calligraphy

Elsa Foyn

Layout

Itzik Yefet

Daniel Weizner

Five Seasons in the Kitchen

Zen Inspired Vegan Cooking

Avital Sebbag

Five Seasons in the Kitchen
Zen Inspired Vegan Cooking

AVITAL SEBBAG

Published by: Avitality, Domain of Change
Translated from Hebrew by: Elizabeth Zauderer

ISBN 978-965-555-927-9

Printed in Israel by: Ravgon Printing House, Ltd.

目錄

TABLE OF CONTENTS

前言

Introduction

This book marks a mile stone on my journey toward an understanding of heathy nutrition and its place in our lives. It is an opportunity for you, dear readers, to glimpse the wonders of a wholesome lifestyle, and to develop an awareness to the mental and spiritual benefits of well-balanced nutrition by experimenting with delicious, easy-to-prepare recipes.

This book motivates change. And change means taking action. Faced with a vast amount of information and approaches to healthy eating, you are probably wondering "What is the right way? " The truth is, there is no "right" way.

I believe with all my heart that we are all creatures of the universe whose earth, seas and skies provide us with the physical, mental and spiritual nourishment we need. That said, we must recognize the values of nature's abundant offerings, and come to know how we can best benefit from them. We must be attuned to nature, to the changing of the seasons, and with each season, to the assortment of foods it provides.

I have been practicing Zen meditation for years, and have visited many Zen monasteries around the globe. During these visits, I found myself drawn to the kitchens, the beating hearts of these establishments, where humble, tasty foods are prepared – foods that satisfy the body, while preserving the ecosystem. The practice of awareness is enhanced when foods are lighter, and so for me Zen cooking is a way to develop the essence of my existence – to contribute to the world by nurturing and nourishing myself and those around me with healthy foods, and by practicing a wholesome, happy, serene and loving lifestyle.

In 1998, I gave birth to my eldest son, the first of five boys. Motherhood radically changed my perspective on life, and deepened my desire for a well-balanced way of life in an ecologically sound environment. As a result, I embarked on an exciting exploration into the wonders of anthropological nutrition, shiatsu, Chinese medicine and Eastern philosophies. It was on these journeys that I came to understand that we are all one with the world, and that nature provides us with all we need to be healthy and happy. It is my hope that this book will encourage you to appreciate nature's gifts, to understand the importance of preserving them, and most importantly, to live your life the best way you can – after all, you too are a gift of nature.

Avital
Song Kuan

GOOD TO KNOW

For information on food products, recommended books and websites, mindful eating, juice cleansing and cooking techniques visit my website at **www.avitality.co.il** or contact me via email: **avitality@gmail.com**

What Is Zen?

By Sefi Rachlevski

禪

The essence of Zen is a striving for truth beyond words; an existential and spiritual truth that any attempt to define distances one further from internalizing its core principle of liberty.

Zen was inspired by existential Taoist philosophy that developed in China approximately 2300 years ago, an age in which Buddhism was established, and in which Plato and Socrates laid the foundations of Western philosophy. This was also the time in which the Hebrew Bible canon of the Second Temple was compiled. The 'tao' in Taoism means 'path;' the leading philosopher of 'the path' was Chang Tzu.

In the following parable Chuang Tzu epitomizes the basic principle of Zen: "If the goat knew it was a goat its feet would become entangled. If the fish knew it was a fish it would sink to the bottom of the river like a lead stone. The goat, the fish, the mountain and the river know themselves by not-knowing. Only man attempts to know himself by way of a knowing. Therefore, man fails to be a man in the same way that a goat is a goat, a fish is a fish, a mountain a mountain and a river-a river."

The constant aspiration for deep knowledge, knowledge that is not founded on knowing, is the foundation of Zen philosophy. This knowledge does not scorn language and intellect, but rather searches for a path beyond definitions and social norms. An existential, internal and personal path, at the end of which is the desired 'enlightenment.' A mystical experience that hauls man out of a myriad of inner, social and definitive conflicts, and restores him to his essential existence, that which is beyond consciousness.

Zen emerged as an existential philosophy some 1500 years ago in China. From there it expanded to Japan, Korea and the rest of the world. Due to its link to Buddhism, Zen was practiced in monasteries where its objectives were to practice deep inner reflection, meditation, personal learning, a humble lifestyle and self- sustenance. Similar to the Hassidic movement at the beginning of its spiritual development, Zen focused on creativity and contemplation through short stories and dialogues. The ability of Zen to release man from his own 'internal well,' the well of words, definitions, social codes, ego, and the physical, is what attracts so many to practice it the world round.

At the opening of Marcel Proust's canonical novel "Remembrance of Things Past," the hero bites into a Madeleine cake. Its taste elicits memories and contemplations that in turn espouse memories that fill the entire novel. It is my hope that through the recipes in this book, each and every reader will find his or her own Madeleine cake. Even if it does not result in an experience of profound enlightenment, engaging with this book will at least constitute a station on a long and pleasurable existential journey of body and soul. At the end of Masehet Kidushin of the Jerusalem Talmud it says: "It is man's future to account for all that he saw and did not eat." Zen experiences itself through non-materiality and non-arrogance, but rather through the satisfying of our deepest, most genuine desires, including our desire for nutrition and nurturing. Delicious and healthy food can fill our lives with the joy of Zen.

Bon appetite!

Sefi Rachlevski

A few years ago I had the amazing opportunity of staying at Avital's home for a few days. Avital is a very vibrant and generous woman! For me, looking at a photo of one of her food creations is similar to looking at Avital, so full of crisp vitality. I was a little concerned that the menu would not contain enough protein or lack taste, but what I experienced was a significant change in how I experienced food – how it was prepared, how it tasted, and how it felt in my body.

Like many of us, I fear that raw and vegan dishes will leave me hungry or dissatisfied. By the time my visit was over, I felt nourished, energetic and grateful to Avital for introducing me to a healthier way of eating.

Zen practice teaches us to rest in the moment in order to allow our mind to open to our innate wisdom and compassion. To rest in the moment does not require any altering of our consciousness or striving for some other state of being. Zen teaches that we already contain the seeds of enlightenment and all we need to do is wake up in just this moment. This awakening allows us to see the beautiful grace and symmetry of this world.

Avital's book is a perfect example of Zen being brought forth into nutrition. Rather than altering and adding to our food, artificially coloring it or cooking the life out of it, Avital shows us how to allow food to be celebrated and honored for what it is in its natural state. We could exchange the word 'food' for the word 'mind'. We meditate to see our original mind. We eat healthy food in order to return to our original balanced and healthy self.

Soeng Hyang
Head Teacher Kwan Um School of Zen

For non-practicing people, food controls the body and the body controls the mind. For practicing people, the mind controls the body and their body controls their food. Eating healthy food just for myself is OK but it will not lead to wisdom. It can be another form of attachment to my body. Eating wisely for others becomes Great Love, Great Compassion and the Great Bodhisattva Way.

Dae Bong Sunim

Dae Bong

Zen describes food in terms of the exquisite harmony and utter simplicity in which individual foods are arranged on the plate to express perfection. For me this was one of my first experiences of Zen – even before I began to practice Zen, I experienced it through the senses. By becoming aware of how food tapped my sense of smell, taste, touch, sound and sight, I experienced that very special "Zen ambience." In this book, Avital has meticulously collected and prepared exquisite recipes to share with us, recipes that engage all the senses and create a unique Zen ambience. Being a sincere student of Zen, I am sure Avital experienced the truth of each of her recipes and has chosen the very best for all of us to share and enjoy.

I wish all of us Zen appetite!

Jo Potter

Ji Do Poep Sa Nim

If you are looking for a book to significantly improve the quality of your life, your health, and your vitality, I highly recommend you read Five Seasons in the Kitchen and be in touch with Avital so your life can be the best life possible.

Joshua Rosenthal

MScEd, Founder/Director, Institute for Integrative Nutrition

Seasons of the Year

The seasons of the year represent change. Movement. The circular progression of time is reflected in the weather, in the color of the sky, in the clouds and intensity of light, in humidity and wind factors. The seasons are stations in time. They bring with them unique sensations associated with smells, textures, colors and flavors. Living in harmony with the seasons means consuming seasonal foods that benefit body, mind and soul for an overall constellation of good health year round.

Spring

春苗

Spring is a time of light breezes, of awakening, motion and creativity. Feeding on sunlight, tiny buds quickly become beautiful blossoms – nature's expression of determination, rejuvenation, cleanliness and growth.

Organ: Liver. Detoxification and rejuvenation.

Color: Green. Stems and leaves contain chlorophyll that cleanses and strengthens body cells.

Flavor: Sour.

Foods: Lemon, vinegar, green apple, blueberry, kiwi, Swiss chard, spinach, cranberry, mallow, kumquat.

Summer

夏种

In summer nature presents itself in all its glory. It is a time of expansion and abundance. Breathtaking spectacles of blossoms and fruits express the potential stored in seeds. We are drawn outdoors to spend time with friends in an atmosphere of sharing, joy and freedom.

Organ: Heart. Communication. Circulation of oxygen - rich blood through the body.

Color: Red.

Taste: Bitter.

Foods: Cherry, watermelon, plum, peach, olives, celery and lettuce leaves, alfalfa sprouts, coffee and tea.

Late Summer

長夏安中

During this transitional season between summer and autumn, the air is humid and dense. The heat is contained and intensified. Fruit rots, and the earth is laden with organic nutrients.

Organ: Spleen-pancreas. Transformation and transportation.

Color: Orange-yellow.

Taste: Sweet.

Foods: Carrot, sweet potato, pumpkin, beet, pear, banana, mango, date, coconut, cinnamon, honey, rice syrup, jams and soups made from ripe fruits.

Autumn

秋收

With light winds and a melancholy atmosphere, autumn marks a beginning and an end. A farewell to summer and the start of a new year. A time of reckoning and promise, a time to let go of the past and plan for the future.

Organ: Lungs. Protection and boundaries.

Color: White.

Taste: Spicy-aromatic.

Foods: Horseradish, radish, kohlrabi, onion, leek, garlic, miso soup.

Winter

冬藏

Winter is a time for slowing down, for introspection and the preservation of body heat. In winter, our ancestors fed on foods collected during summer and autumn. As the days get shorter and the cold sets in, more time is dedicated to meditation, and to appreciating the quiet and stillness.

Organ: Kidneys. Body wisdom. Ancestral energies.

Color: Blue.

Taste: Salty.

Foods: Soy sauce, seaweed, root vegetables, lentils, stews, soups, sea salt.

春苗

In spring wind
Peach blossoms
Begin to come apart.
Doubts do not grow
Branches and leaves.

Zen Master Dogen

SPRING

目錄

Spring

PAPAYA PLUS SMOOTHIE

材料

Yields 2 liters

1/4 papaya

6 strawberries

1 green apple

3 dates, pitted

2 celery stalks

4 lettuce leaves

4 sprigs mint

5 almonds or walnuts

1 Tbs. coconut oil

4 cups cold water

5 ice cubes

super-food additive (10 chlorella tablets or 1 tsp. spirulina powder, 1 tsp. ground cocoa beans or 2 whole cocoa beans)

Rinse fruits and vegetables and dice. Place in a blender, add water and process to a smooth silky consistency. For desired consistency, add or decrease amount of water.

Japanese Pickles

Thoroughly rinse vegetables. Cut cucumbers and carrots into rounds. Cut the remaining vegetables into cubes. In a bowl, combine vegetables with garlic, ginger root and dill. In a separate bowl, mix pickling liquid ingredients. Pour over vegetables. Marinate for 1 hour to absorb flavors.

GOOD TO KNOW

Radishes help strengthen the lungs, cleanse the kidneys, neutralize toxins and boost the immune system. This recipe was inspired by the late Irit Muzan, a talented and dear friend.

材料

Yields 1 kg.

2 cucumbers

2 carrots

2 red bell peppers

2 kohlrabi

2 radishes

3 cloves garlic, crushed

2 Tbs. fresh ginger root, grated

Pickling liquid

2 Tbs. soy sauce

2 tsp. sesame oil

1 Tbs. sesame seeds

1 cup dill, chopped

2 cups water

1 Tbs. Umeboshi sauce

1 Tbs. rice vinegar

Vegetable Stuffed Persimmon Fruit Leather in Asian Paste

材料

Yields 8 rolls

8 10x10 cm. sheets persimmon fruit leather or Nori sheet

1 bunch chives

1 zucchini

1 carrot

1 avocado

1 red bell pepper

1 handful sunflower sprouts

250 gr. assorted mushrooms

1 red onion

mung bean sprouts

1 bunch coriander

Paste

1/2 cup soy sauce

2 Tbs. sesame oil

2 Tbs. lemon juice

1 Tbs. olive oil

1 Thai chili pepper

1/4 cup cashews

Persimmon fruit leather

Rinse and peel 5 persimmons. In a food processor, process into a fully combined spread. Spread in thin layers on Teflex sheets and dry in a food dehydrator for 10 hours at 40°C. Alternatively, buy ready-made leather (available at health food stores).

Paste

Process all sauce ingredients in a food processor until smooth and fully combined.

Rolls

Julienne vegetables. Spread a tablespoon of sauce across the center of each leather sheet. Arrange vegetables on top of sauce. Roll sheets and serve.

GOOD TO KNOW

The Goji berry is a tropical fruit containing a high level of anti-oxidants. Its therapeutic properties include boosting the immune system, fortifying the liver and improving blood flow. The Goji berry is rich in vitamins, iron and 18 amino acids. Its tart flavor and bright red color add a unique taste and freshness to a wide variety of dishes.

Fresh Tabbouleh Salad

材料

Serves 4

1 cup coarsely ground bulgur or quinoa

2 cups arugula (rocket)

2 celery stalks

2 cups parsley, chopped

2 lemons, peeled and chopped

1 lime, peeled and chopped

1 cup Goji berries

1/2 cup mint, chopped

1/4 cup olive oil

1 tsp. coarse Atlantic sea salt

Soak bulgur or quinoa in water for 1 hour. Rinse and dry. Rinse vegetables and chop. Mix all ingredients in a salad bowl. Serve.

Spring Tofu Sandwich

材料

Serves 1

2 slices sour dough bread (recipe on page 50)

100 gr. tofu

1/4 cup soy sauce

1/2 cup water

1/2 ground black pepper

1 radish

1/4 cup sunflower sprouts

3 sprigs coriander

1 tsp. Indian Pesto (recipe on page 98)

Preheat oven to 180°C. Cut tofu into 1/2 cm. thick slices and arrange on a baking pan. Pour soy sauce and water over tofu. Bake for 15 minutes or until liquids evaporate. Cool and refrigerate. Cut peppers and radish into long, narrow strips. Chop sprouts and coriander. Spread both slices of bread with pesto. Arrange tofu on one slice. Top with vegetables, herbs and the second slice of bread.

GOOD TO KNOW

Tofu is produced from soy beans in the form of a large cheese-like lump. It is used as a substitute for animal protein, and is especially popular in Japanese and Korean monasteries where diets are vegetarian. For maximum nutritional value, it is recommended to use fermented, non-genetically modified tofu. Naturally bland in taste, tofu absorbs the flavors of your choice.

Green Bean and Snow Pea Salad
with Purple Cabbage

春

材料

Serves 4

Salad

1 cup green beans

1 cup snow peas

1/4 purple cabbage

4 cherry or
sun-dried tomatoes

50 gr. tofu

1 tsp. soy sauce

Dressing

juice from 1 lemon

1 Tbs. olive oil

1 tsp. dried hyssop

1/2 tsp. coarse
Atlantic sea salt

Rinse all vegetables thoroughly. Stem beans and snow peas and cut into thin slices. Cut tofu into small cubes and place in a bowl. Add soy sauce and marinate for 10 minutes to absorb flavors. Chop cabbage and combine with tofu, beans and snow peas. Add tomatoes and dressing. Toss and serve.

Oven-Dried Tomatoes: Halve 2 kg. cherry tomatoes. Using a spoon, discard seeds. Arrange tomatoes, skin side down, on a baking pan lined with parchment paper. Sprinkle with salt and a pinch of oregano or thyme. Dry in an oven preheated to 80°C for 8-12 hours. If using a food hydrator, dry at 41°C for 24 hours.

To preserve: arrange tomatoes in a glass jar, cover with olive oil and refrigerate.

GOOD TO KNOW

According to Macrobiotic principles, selenium vegetables such as tomatoes are considered poisonous. Therefore, in this recipe, I substitute fresh tomatoes with sun-dried tomatoes. Though vitamins are lost in the drying process, the tomato's lycopene content – a highly effective anti-oxidant – becomes more readily available. I dry tomatoes in a food dehydrator and preserve them in olive oil. A regular oven will also do the trick.

Spring Pyramid with Artichoke

材料

Serves 4

Salad

2 artichokes

2 Swiss chard leaves

6 spinach leaves

2 scallions

2 celery stalks

1 avocado

1 red bell pepper

1/4 cup parsley
or dill

1 cup pistachios

Dressing

2 tsp. Japanese radish,
grated

juice from 1 lemon

juice from 1 orange

1/2 tsp. sesame oil

1 tsp. soy sauce

1/2 tsp. coarse
Atlantic sea salt

Cook artichokes in boiling water for 30 minutes. Cool and remove leaves. Using a paring knife or spoon, remove fuzzy fibers from artichoke hearts. Cut hearts into eights. Thoroughly rinse vegetables. Finely chop Swiss chard, spinach, scallion, red pepper and celery. Peel avocado and dice. Mix vegetables in a bowl, add parsley or dill and pistachios. Put all dressing ingredients in a jar with a tight fitting lid. Shake untill fully combined. Stack vegetables on individual plates to create a pyramid. Pour dressing over vegetables. Serve.

GOOD TO KNOW

Artichokes are rich in dietary fibers that help cleanse the liver, gall bladder and intestines. Fresh or cooked, artichokes make a delicious and healthy snack.

Spring Soba Noodle Salad

材料

Serves 4

1 package (250 gr.) soba noodles gluten free

2 Tbs. sesame oil

2 heads broccoli

1 medium sized cauliflower

1 cup arugula (rocket)

1 cup purple string beans

3 scallions

1 chili pepper

1 Tbs. soy sauce

Garnish

1 Tbs. black sesame seeds

juice from 1 lemon

Cook noodles according to manufacturer's directions; make sure not to overcook. Rinse in cold water, drain, add 1 Tbs. sesame oil and cool. Fill a large bowl with lukewarm water. Add 1 Tbs. salt and soak broccoli, cauliflower and arugula (rocket) for 15 minutes. Remove and drain.

Divide cauliflower and broccoli into florets. Snap tips off beans and cut into quarters. Slice scallions and chili pepper into thin strips. Combine all ingredients in a serving dish. Season with sesame oil and soy sauce. Toss gently. Sprinkle with sesame seeds and drizzle with lemon juice to taste.

GOOD TO KNOW

Soba is Japanese for spelt, or "kasha" in Eastern Europe. Spelt grains' dominant flavor and smell do not appeal to everyone. Soba noodles, on the other hand, do not have a distinctive smell and are great served in warm or cold salads.

WHOLE BASMATI RICE WITH HIJIKI

材料

Serves 4

500 gr. whole Basmati rice

1/4 cup Hijiki

2 Tbs. olive oil

1 onion, finely chopped

1 tsp. curry powder

1 tsp. coarse Atlantic sea salt

4 cups water

Garnish

1 cucumber, finely chopped

1/2 cup dill, rinsed and chopped

Soak rice in water for several hours (to reduce cooking time). Add Hijiki to the water 15 minutes before draining. Drain and rinse until water runs clear. Dry.

Heat olive oil in a wide, deep sauce pan. Add onions and sauté till golden. Add curry, stir and sauté for 1 minute. Add rice, salt and water. Bring to the boil, reduce heat and cook covered for 40 minutes. Drain and arrange rice on a serving dish. Garnish with chopped cucumbers and dill.

GOOD TO KNOW

Basmati rice is a highly satisfying grain rich in soluble fibers that help cleanse the digestive system. Containing vitamin E, the grain's sprouts help retain vitality, delay aging and cleanse tissue cells. Hijiki is rich in iodine and vitamin B12.

Rye and Spelt Flour Sicilian Pizza

材料

Yields 20 individual pizzas

Dough

1 kg. spelt flour

500 gr. rye flour

1 cup olive oil

2 Tbs. dry yeast

or 1 cup of sourdough

2-3 cups lukewarm water

1 tsp. coarse Atlantic sea salt

1 tsp. maple syrup

Vegetable Topping

10 sun-dried tomatoes

12 zucchini, cut into thin rounds

1 eggplant, cut into thin rounds

1 onion, thinly sliced

olive oil

oregano

coarse Atlantic sea salt

3 red bell peppers

100 gr. pumpkin, peeled

Macadamia nut cheese (recipe on page 170)

Tomato Sauce

2 Tbs. olive oil

1 onion, finely chopped

4 cloves garlic, crushed

5 tomatoes, finely chopped

2 cups water

100 gr. tomato paste

1 tsp. coarse Atlantic sea salt

1 tsp. black pepper

fresh oregano, finely chopped

fresh basil, finely chopped

Dough

Combine all ingredients to make a warm, elastic dough. Knead for at least 10 minutes. Cover with a towel and set to rise in a warm place until double in size. Divide dough into ping-pong ball sized portions.

Vegetable topping

Preheat oven to 250°C. Arrange zucchini, eggplant and onion slices on a baking pan lined with parchment paper. Brush with olive oil and sprinkle with oregano and salt. Bake for 15 minutes.

Tomato Sauce

In a pan, sweat onion in olive oil until golden. Add garlic and stir. Add tomatoes and cook until soft. Add water, tomato paste, salt and pepper and cook on low heat for 15 minutes. Add herbs and cook for an additional 15 minutes. Transfer sauce to food processer and process till smooth.

Assemble Pizza

Lower oven heat to 200°C. Roll out balls of dough as thinly as possible. Evenly spread tomato sauce, top with vegetables and Bake for 15 minutes.

Dough-free Asparagus Quiche

材料

26 cm. pie dish or 6 individual 6 cm. pie dishes

1 bunch asparagus

2 leeks

1 cup olive oil

10 Kalamata olives, pitted

10 sun-dried tomatoes

1 bunch basil

3 cloves garlic, crushed

2 cups Macadamia nut cheese (recipe on page 170)

salt and pepper

sesame seeds

Preheat oven to 180°C. Scald asparagus in boiling water for 2 minutes. Cut into 4 cm. slices and place in a mixing bowl. Cut leeks into rounds and sweat in 1 Tbs. olive oil in a pan. Add leeks to bowl. Chop olives, tomatoes and basil. Add to bowl with garlic.

In a separate bowl, add olive oil, Macadamia nut cheese, salt and pepper and mix. Pour mixture over vegetables and combine till fully coated. Transfer to pie dish or individual dishes. Sprinkle with sesame seeds. Bake for 20 minutes. Lower heat to 140°C and bake for an additional 25 minutes.

GOOD TO KNOW

Most of us are familiar with exclusive varieties of asparagus sold in supermarkets and vegetable markets. There is however another option—a wild, non-cultivated variety that grows in Israel's natural groves throughout the spring. Similar in shape, but thinner than the cultivated variety, wild asparagus is crispy and can be eaten fresh. Asparagus's dark green color is indicative of its high chlorophyll content that is exceptionally beneficial for cleansing the liver and dissolving kidney stones.

Spring Vegetable and Shallot Pie

材料

26 cm. pie dish or
6 individual 6 cm.
pie dishes

Dough

2 cups spelt flour

1/2 cup olive oil

1/2 cup cashews, chopped

1/2 cup water

1 tsp. lemon juice

Filling

3 Tbs. olive oil

2 shallots, chopped

4 King Oyster mushrooms, chopped

1 head broccoli

2 cups spinach

1 cup olive oil

500 gr. Macadamia nut cheese (recipe on page 170)

5 basil leaves

3 cloves garlic, crushed

salt and pepper

Dough

Mix spelt flour and olive oil until fully incorporated. Add cashews, water and lemon juice and mix. If necessary, add water to make a smooth dough. Cover and refrigerate for 30 minutes.

Filling

Heat olive oil in a wide pan. Sweat shallots. Add mushrooms and sweat for 5 minutes. Scald broccoli in boiling water for 2 minutes and cut into thin slices. In a bowl, mix olive oil, Macadamia nut cheese, basil, garlic and spices. Combine with mushrooms and broccoli.

Preheat oven to 180°C. Roll out the dough and place in the pie dish, pressing it evenly into the bottom and sides. Perforate dough with a fork. Pour in filling. Bake for 20 minutes. Reduce heat to 140°C and bake for an additional 25 minutes.

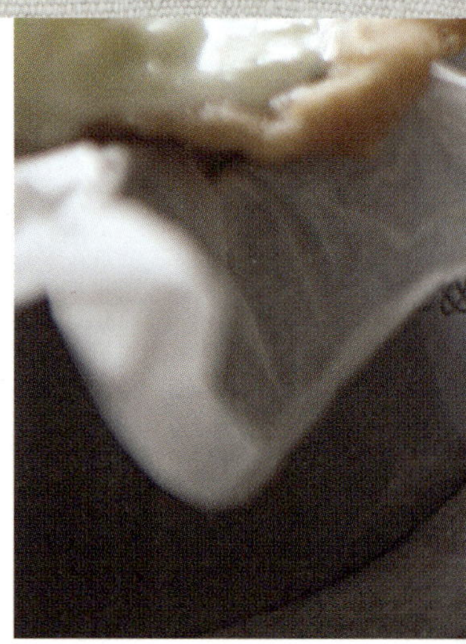

Carrot Soup with a Hint of Coconut

材料

Serves 6

6 carrots

4 small parsley roots or 1 large, quarted

1 celery root, peeled

2 leeks

1 onion

3 cloves garlic

1 celery stalk

3 Tbs. coconut oil

1 tsp. black pepper

1 Tbs. coarse Atlantic sea salt

3 liters water

Garnish

1 Tbs. black sesame seeds

1/4 cup broccoli or mung bean sprouts

Rinse carrots and parsley roots thoroughly (if organic, no need to peel). Cube carrots, parsley and celery roots. Cut leeks and onion into rounds. In a large pot, sweat leeks and onions in coconut oil. Add carrots, roots, spices and 3 liters water. Bring to the boil, reduce heat and simmer for 1 hour. Using a hand blender, puree soup until smooth and silky. Pour into soup bowls. Garnish with sesame seeds and sprouts. Serve.

GOOD TO KNOW

Sprouts are a healthy substitute for croutons. They contain enzymes that help cleanse the body's cells. Lentils and seeds can be easily sprouted at home using a colander, canvas sprouting bag, glass jar, tiered or electric sprouter. I recommend starting out with legumes such as mung beans or lentils that are easy to sprout.

JOJA'S SOURDOUGH BREAD

材料

Sourdough Starter

10 raisins

1 cup water

4 cups lukewarm water

5 cups spelt flour

Bread

2 loaf pans

1 cup starter

1 kg. spelt flour

1 Tbs. salt

1/4 cup olive oil

1 1/2 liters lukewarm water

Optional Additions

1 cup oats, raisins, prunes, olives

Sourdough Starter

1. Soak raisins in 1 cup water for 8 hours at room temperature. In a bowl, combine soaking liquid and 1 cup flour. Transfer to a jar and cover with cheesecloth. Keep at room temperature for 1 day.

2. On the second day, add 1 cup each of flour and water to the starer jar, once a day for 3 days. On the fourth day your sourdough starter is ready to use. Best kept refregerated.

3. Your starter needs weekly "feeding" by adding a cup each of flower and water or by replacing the amount of starter used for baking. Make sure to have at least 2 cups starter in your fridge at all times.

Bread

Lightly grease loaf pans with olive oil. Mix all ingredients including starter. Pour into pans, filling up to 3/4 from top. Using a wet spoon or spatula, smooth surface. Cover with a towel and let rise in a warm place for 5-6 hours, depending on the season.

Heat oven to 250°C. Bake 10 minutes, reduce heat to 180°C and bake for an additional hour or when loaf sounds hollow when tapping.

Remove loaves from pans, cover with a towel and cool on a rack.

GOOD TO KNOW

Sourdough is like a living organism, in need of constant care and nutrition. As a primary ingredient that is traditionally passed on from one baker to another, sourdough has evolved into many varieties, each of which carries a unique personal story.

My sourdough starter originated in a Korean monastery in Hungary. While visiting there, I was served wonderfully flavored bread, and so I asked the cook, a Polish nun named Bulchawa Han Zanim, for the recipe. She gladly shared the recipe and a portion of her starter with me. This particular starter, she explained, was given to her by her Polish friend Joja, who had received it from a friend of hers.

PERSIMMON SORBET | GRANOLA AND MAPLE SYRUP COOKIES

材料

Persimmon Sorbet

Yields 500 ml.

1 kg. ripe persimmons

juice from 4 oranges

1 Tbs. coconut oil

1/4 cup maple syrup

1/2 cup pecans

Granola and Maple Syrup Cookies

Yields 10-20 cookies

2 cups granola

1/4 cup coconut oil

3/4 cup spelt flour

1/2 cup maple syrup

2 Tbs. flax seeds, soaked

Optional

zest from 1/4 lemon

shredded coconut

sugar-free, store bought granola with dried fruit

Sorbet

Combine all ingredients in a blender until fully incorporated and smooth. Pour mixture into a divided silicon mold of your choice (triangles, hearts, etc.). Freeze. Sorbet can be served with a granola cookie (see recipe below), and garnished with bittersweet chocolate shavings.

Cookies

Preheat oven to 180°C. Combine and mix all ingredients into a sticky batter (do not add flour). Using a tablespoon, scoop portions onto a baking pan lined with parchment paper. No need to flatten, the batter will spread while baking. Bake for 15 minutes until golden, or for 24 hours in a food dehydrator at 41°C.

GOOD TO KNOW

Persimmons are rich in nutritional fibers, vitamin A, beta-carotene and anti-oxidants. In Chinese medicine, persimmons and other orange fruits and vegetables, are considered especially effective in boosting the digestive system. This sorbet can be made with other fruits that ripen in the spring, preferably those with dense textures such as mango, papaya, banana and even avocado.

When preparing pastries, cakes and cookies, I recommend substituting sugar with natural sweeteners. I prefer organic maple syrup, rice malt, molasses, honey or sugar-free date honey.

夏种

ALL THIS RIPENESS,
IN OUR BEDS, FIGS,
DATES,
WATERMELON,
GRAPES,
MULBERRIES.
SUMMER LOVE.

SEFI RACHLEVSKI

SUMMER

目錄

Summer

Pomegranate and Lime Drink

材料

Yields 2 cups

2 pomegranates or 2 tsp. natural pomegranate syrup

2 kobo (tropical fruit)

1 lime

2 pears

1 cup mint leaves

1 tsp. hemp oil

Juice pomegranates into clear juice. Peel lime and kobo. Thoroughly rinse mint leaves and pears. In a heavy duty juicer, process pears and mint into a clear, fiber-free juice. Mix with pomegranate juice and hemp oil.

GOOD TO KNOW

Hemp oil is produced from the part of cannabis seeds that do not contain significant amounts of the psychoactive element tetrahydrocannabinol (THC). The seeds contain a high concentration (80%) of fatty acids. Hemp oil is rich in anti-oxidants, helps reduce risks for cancer and heart diseases, boosts energy and contributes to weight loss. It is recommended to consume hemp oil daily.

Endive Boats Stuffed with Macadamia Feta

材料

Serves 8

12 endives, (preferably with wide leaves)

Stuffing

100 gr. Macadamia nuts

6 Kalamata olives, pitted

4 sun-dried tomatoes

1/4 cup chopped coriander

water (as needed)

Garnish

1/4 cup sesame seeds

8 basil leaves

8 beet juliennes

1 Tbs. olive oil

Rinse endive thoroughly. Gently separate leaves. In a food processor, combine all stuffing ingredients into a coarse, thick paste. Add water as needed. Form stuffing into small balls using a Parisian spoon or tablespoon. Roll balls in sesame seeds. Place a basil leaf in each endive "boat" followed by a ball of stuffing. Garnish with beet juliennes. Drizzle with olive oil (optional).

Asparagus Wrapped in Seaweed
with Tofu and Lemon Crumbs

Steam asparagus in bamboo steamer for exactly 3 minutes or blanch in boiling water. Roast almonds in a hot skillet with a drizzle of olive oil and salt, or in a food hydrator at 41°C for 5 hours. Dice tofu and marinate in soy sauce for 10 minutes. Place asparagus on a serving dish. Wrap each asparagus sprig with a slice of Nori. Arrange tofu cubes on top of asparagus and dress with lemon juice and olive oil. Sprinkle with almonds, and drizzle with tahini. Garnish with radish sprouts. Serve immediately.

材料

Serves 4-6

1 bunch asparagus

100 gr. peeled almonds

200 gr. tofu

2 Tbs. soy sauce

1 Nori sheet,
cut into thin slices

juice from 1 lemon

1/4 cup olive oil

3 Tbs. tahini paste

1 cup radish sprouts

1 liter water

Beet Pillows Stuffed with Almond-Sprout Spread

材料

Serves 4

2 large beets

1 bunch parsley

handful broccoli sprouts

Stuffing

1 cup almonds, soaked in lukewarm water for 12 hours

1 Tbs. tahini paste

1/4 ginger root

1 jalapeño pepper

2 cloves garlic

juice from 1/2 a lemon

1 Tbs. Umeboshi sauce

1/2 cup water

1/2 tsp. black pepper

To serve

1 Tbs. olive oil

1 Tbs. lemon juice

Peel beets. Cut into thin slices and soak in water for 1 hour. Chop parsley. In a food processor, process all stuffing ingredients for 3 minutes into a smooth spread.

Arrange beet slices on a serving dish. Place 1 tsp. almond spread onto half the amount of slices. Garnish with chopped parsley, cover with a beet slice and repeat. In a small bowl, mix olive oil and lemon juice. Pour over beets. Garnish with broccoli sprouts.

GOOD TO KNOW

Beets can be eaten cooked or raw. Raw beets should be soaked in a pickling solution such as brine or lemon juice. This recipe is a vegan variation on ravioli. To slice beets, I recommend using a mandolin set at desired thickness.

Roasted Eggplant in Tahini Paste

GOOD TO KNOW

Eggplants are acidic, so I recommend consuming small quantities as appetizers or side dishes.

Roast eggplant on an open fire (BBQ, grill or stove) until scorched on all sides. Cool. Remove skin, leaving cap and stem attached. In a small bowl, mix ginger, garlic, soy sauce and pepper. Place eggplant on a serving dish. Pour dressing over eggplant, drizzle with tahini paste and sprinkle with sesame.

材料

Serves 1-2

1 eggplant

1/2 ginger root, grated

2 cloves garlic, grated

2 tsp. soy sauce

1/2 tsp. black pepper

2 tsp. tahini paste

2 tsp. sesame seeds

Tahini paste is available in multiple varieties. I recommend using Ethiopian tahini, made from sprouted, whole organic sesame in a cold press process. This tahini is dark in color, and has a bitter sweet taste developed through the sprouting of seeds. Sprouting also accounts for high levels of enzymes and oxalic acid that enhance body cells' absorption of calcium and other vital minerals.

Baked Cauliflower

Soak cauliflower in a bowl of salt water for 1 hour. Drain and brush with olive oil. Sprinkle with salt and herbs. Preheat oven at 100°C. Wrap cauliflower in parchment paper and bake for 20 minutes. Remove parchment paper, turn cauliflower over and bake for an additional 20 minutes.

材料

Serves 4

1 whole cauliflower

1 Tbs. olive oil

1 tsp. coarse Atlantic sea salt

Herbs to taste (thyme, oregano, rosemary)

GOOD TO KNOW

Soaking vegetables in salt water (or a water-vinegar solution) helps get rid of insects.

Baked Vegetable Chips

Rinse vegetables thoroughly. Dry and cut into thin slices using a mandolin or vegetable peeler.

Sweet Potato Chips

Arrange slices on a flat baking pan. Cover with water, add apple vinegar and marinate for 15 minutes. Drain. Brush with olive oil and sprinkle with sea salt and chili powder. See baking instructions below.

Beet Chips

Arrange slices on baking pan lined with parchment paper or on a food dehydrator pan lined with a sheet of non stick Teflex. Brush with olive oil and sprinkle with salt. See baking instructions below.

Zucchini Chips

Arrange slices on a flat baking pan lined with parchment paper or a food dehydrator pan lined with a sheet of non stick Teflex. Brush with olive oil and sprinkle with salt and Italian herbs. See baking instructions below.

Baking

Food dehydrator: dry for 4 hours on Teflex. Remove Teflex. Turn chips over and dry for an additional 6-8 hours.

Oven: preheat oven at 100°C. Bake for 1 hour. Turn chips over and bake for an additional hour.

材料

Yields 300 gr.

1 beet

1 sweet potato

3 zucchini

1 Tbs. olive oil

2 Tbs. water

1 tsp. apple vinegar

1 Tbs. coarse Atlantic sea salt

1/2 tsp. chili powder

1 tsp. mixed Italian herbs (oregano, thyme, basil)

THREE WAY TOASTINI

材料

Yields 6

6 slices rye bread

1 Tbs. Indian Pesto
(recipe on pg 98)

1 Tbs. Sun-dried Tomato, Walnuts and Ginger Spread
(recipe on pg 98)

1 Tbs. Sprouted Lentil and Walnut Spread
(recipe on pg 98)

6 slices tofu, marinated in soy sauce for 5 minutes

3 sun-dried tomatoes, thinly sliced

3 Champignon mushrooms, thinly sliced

Garnish

1 cucumber, diced

1/2 cup dill, chopped

Preheat oven to 200°C. (roast or grill setting). Spread each slice of bread with one of the spreads. Top with tofu, tomatoes and mushrooms. Arrange on a baking pan lined with parchment paper. Grill for 15 minutes.

GOOD TO KNOW

According to Chinese medicine, scorched-grilled flavors are characteristic of summer. Toastini is an excellent appetizer or light meal. The tofu can be substituted with Macadamia nut cheese (see recipe on page 170) or any other variety of vegan cheese.

GREEN SALAD WITH MUSTARD MISO DRESSING

材料

Serves 4

1 bunch assorted lettuce

1 bunch Turkish spinach

Dressing

1 Tbs. light miso

1 tsp. mustard

1/2 tsp. black pepper

1 Tbs. olive oil

juice from 1 lemon

Rinse spinach and lettuce thoroughly. Dry in a lettuce spinner. Gently tear leaves, and arrange in a salad bowl. Combine dressing ingredients, and pour over leaves before serving. Garnish with edible flowers such as pansies.

Asian Papaya Salad

GOOD TO KNOW

I was first introduced to papaya salad by a Thai woman named Nowi. Nowi worked in my kitchen for two years. The original recipe is made with green papaya and cherry tomatoes only, and the dressing is based on fish sauce. In this version, I substitute fish sauce with a combination of sesame and Nigella oils.

Peel carrots, beet and papaya. Cut into juliennes using a food processor or julienne peeler. Transfer to serving dish. Chop chestnuts and coriander. Add to vegetables. Combine dressing ingredients and pour over salad.

材料

Serves 4

Salad

2 carrots

1 beet

1 green papaya

1 cup chestnuts, peeled

1/2 cup coriander leaves

Dressing

juice from 1 lime

1 tsp. chili oil

1 tsp. coarse Atlantic sea salt

1 tsp. sesame oil

1 tsp. Nigella seed oil

Black Rice Noodles and Kohlrabi

材料

Serves 4

1 package (250 gr.) black rice noodles

2 kohlrabi

2 scallions

1 cup mixed herbs: coriander, parsley, dill

1 tsp. coarse Atlantic sea salt

Dressing

1 piece ginger root (to taste)

1 Tbs. soy sauce

juice from 1 lemon

1 Tbs. sesame oil

1 tsp. black pepper

Cook rice noodles according to manufacturer's instructions. Drain, rinse and cool. Cut scallions into rounds. Soak herbs in lukewarm water with 1 tsp. salt for 15 minutes. Rinse, dry and chop. Peel kohlrabi and julienne using julienne knife or food processor. In a mixing bowl, combine noodles, kohlrabi, scallions and herbs. Grate ginger into a separate bowl. Add soy sauce, sesame oil, lemon juice and pepper. Whisk until fully combined. Pour over noodles, mix and serve.

GOOD TO KNOW

Black rice noodles are made from black rice flour, and are commonly used in Asian cuisine. Because they do not contain gluten (found in wheat flour), rice noodles are a delicious solution for people with celiac disease or sensitive to gluten.

Squash Flowers Stuffed with Mushrooms, Asparagus and Pine Nuts

Preheat oven to 180°C. In a pan, sauté red onion in 1 tsp. olive oil until browned. Chop mushrooms and asparagus. Add to pan with garlic and herbs and sauté for 5 minutes. Cool. Roast pine nuts in a pan or in a food dehydrator for 3 hours. Cool and add to mushroom mixture with Macadamia nut cheese and chives. Open squash flowers gently, discard pollen and stuff with vegetable stuffing. Pinch and twist flowers to close hermetically. Roll flowers in batter. Place on a baking pan lined with parchment paper and bake for 30 minutes.

Dressing

Chop onions and sauté in olive oil until browned. Dice tomatoes. Add to onions with garlic and seasonings. Sauté for 15 minutes. Add 1/2 cup water and simmer for an additional 10 minutes. Transfer to food processor and process till fully combined. Pour over stuffed flowers. Top with Macadamia nut cheese. Serve.

材料

Serves 4

1 red onion, chopped

12 fresh squash flowers

250 gr. assorted mushrooms

1/2 bunch asparagus

2 cloves garlic

50 gr. pine nuts

1 cup Macadamia nut cheese (recipe on pg 170)

2 Tbs. chives, chopped

1 Tbs. olive oil

1/2 tsp. black pepper

1 tsp. coarse Atlantic sea salt

1/4 cup fresh oregano

Batter

1 cup spelt bread crumbs

1 cup coconut oil

Dressing

1 onion

4 tomatoes

1 clove garlic

1 tsp. oregano

1 tsp. coarse Atlantic sea salt

GOOD TO KNOW

Squash flowers are not only beautiful to look at, they're considered the ultimate gourmet ingredient. It's no wonder world renown chefs celebrate their arrival in the autumn by adding them to a wide variety of recipes. Stuffed with vegetables, squash flowers are undoubtedly one of the most delicious delicacies imaginable.

Shosh Caviat's Hummus and Broad Bean Special

材料

Serves 10

Hummus Spread

500 gr. dry chickpeas

1 tsp. cumin

100 gr. tahini paste

juice from 2 lemons

2 tsp. olive oil

1 tsp. coarse
Atlantic sea salt

4-6 cloves garlic

water, as needed
(reserve chickpea
cooking liquid)

Broad Bean Stew

500 gr. dry
broad beans

juice from 2 lemons

2 onions, chopped

4 cloves garlic, chopped

4 Tbs. olive oil

1 tsp. salt

1 tsp. black pepper

1 tsp. chili pepper

2 liters water

Hummus Spread

Soak chickpeas in water for 8 hours. Rinse thoroughly, drain and leave in colander for 8 hours until they begin to sprout. Transfer sprouted chickpeas to a pressure cooker. Add water to cover (approx. 1 cm. above chickpeas). Cook for 1 hour. If using a regular pot, cook for 2 hours.

Drain chickpeas. Reserve liquid. In a food processor, process chickpeas while gradually adding tahini paste, juice from one lemon and garlic. Season with salt, cumin and olive oil. Process for approximately 15 minutes to desired consistency. Texture depends on the amount of time processed, while thickness is determined by the amount of cooking liquids added.

Broad Bean Stew

Soak beans in water for 8 hours. Cook in a pressure cooker for 1 hour, or in a regular pot for 1 1/2 hours until beans are soft. In a pan, sweat onions in 1 tsp. olive oil until golden. Add garlic and stir. Add beans, lemon juice and the remaining olive oil. Season with salt and pepper. Stir until fully combined.

To Serve

Spread hummus evenly on a flat plate. Add 2 Tbs. broad bean mixture. Sprinkle with sweet paprika and dried hyssop (optional) and drizzle with olive oil. Serve with lemon juice and zhug (hot pepper paste).

GOOD TO KNOW

Home-made hummus spread is easy to make. Unlike store bought hummus, it does not contain preservatives and so does not keep for long. I recommend making small quantities at a time.

On a personal note: Shosh Caviat was my close friend for over thirty years.From the time I left my parents' house and moved into my own home, until she passed away, she treated me like a daughter. She taught me the basics of cooking, shared many tips for working in the kitchen, but most importantly, Shosh taught me not to be afraid. On Saturdays her home was filled with family and friends who gathered around her table to savor an abundance of homemade salads. Shosh's guests especially enjoyed dipping fresh yeman pita bread in hummus and broad bean stew, accompanied by a fresh green leaf and onion salad.

GOOD TO KNOW

I was first introduced to this recipe at the "Pure Food and Wine" restaurant in New York City. Based on sprouted lentils, it is a variation on Samara's (a visionary leader of the raw food school) original version.

Baked Falafel

Soak lentils in water for 8 hours. Rinse and place in a colander or sprouting bag for 24 hours. Rinse with water every 2 hours - lentils will produce tiny green sprouts. Transfer to a food processor, add remaining falafel ingredients and process till fully combined. Form balls from mixture. Arrange on a baking pan lined with parchment paper. Press each ball gently. Bake in an oven preheated to 180°C for 20 minutes, or in a food dehydrator at 40°C for 8-10 hours.

Dressing

Process all ingredients in a food processor until fully combined and smooth. Serve aside falafel balls. Optional: serve with pita bread.

材料

Yields 25 balls

Falafel Mixture

1 cup sprouted green lentils

1 cup almonds, soaked in water for 12 hours

1 cup cashews, soaked in water for 12 hours

1/2 cup ground fresh flax seed

1/4 cup sesame seeds

1 cup chopped parsley

1/4 tsp. coarse Atlantic sea salt

1 Tbs. lemon juice

3 cloves garlic

1 tsp. cumin

2 Tbs. olive oil

1 Tbs. water (or more)

Dressing

4 Tbs. tahini paste

2 tomatoes

1 bunch parsley

juice from 1 lemon

1 tsp. coarse Atlantic sea salt

LADY FINGERS

材料

Serves 4

500 gr. Sambal Asian okra

1 large onion

6 cloves garlic

6 tomatoes

1 tsp. coarsely ground black pepper

1 tsp. turmeric

1 1/2 Tbs. coarse Atlantic sea salt

1 Tbs. coconut oil

Stem and rinse okra. Place on paper towel and dry in the sun for 30 minutes. Chop onion, garlic and tomatoes. In a wok or deep pan, stir fry onion with coconut oil until browned. Add tomatoes, garlic and spices. Stir fry for 5 minutes. Add okra and bring to the boil. Cover partially, lower flame and simmer for 1 hour.

Serve on a bed of whole rice, quinoa or pearl barley.

On one of my visits to my dear friend Nadav, my personal organic farmer from Givat Olga, he introduced me to an exceptionally long and delicious variety of okra grown by the Thai farmers working on the farm. Until then, I had no idea just how tasty raw okra can be.

GOOD TO KNOW

Okra is available throughout the summer. There are numerous types of okra, the most common of which is the small (2-3 cm. long) variety. The mucilage found in okra protects the intestines. Okra also helps balance sugar levels.

Nut Ice Cream Nuggets

夏种

Base

In a food processor, coarsely ground all ingredients. Press mixture into the bottom of the pie dish. The base should be about 1 cm. high and even.

Cream Filling

In a blender, blend all filling ingredients until smooth. Pour filling onto base. Freeze for 3 hours to stabilize. Cut pie into small nuggets. Serve.

材料

26 cm. pie dish

Base

3 cups assorted nuts (Macadamia, Brazil, walnut, pecan, almonds)

20 dates, pitted

1/2 cup coconut oil

Cream Filling

juice and zest from 1 lemon

2 cups cashews, soaked in water for 12 hours

3 Tbs. maple syrup

1 cup water

1 tsp. vanilla extract

1 Tbs. cocoa powder

GOOD TO KNOW

Nut based ice creams and other frozen desserts are very popular in the vegan kitchen. But you don't have to be a vegan to enjoy these egg, flour and milk-free desserts. Even the cocoa powder can be substituted with vanilla extract and lemon.

長夏安中

ORANGE AND SWEET.
INTOXICATING SCENT
ON THE BREEZE AMIDST THE LEAVES
SH...SH...SH...
MOTHER EARTH
RESTING.

AVITAL SEBBAG

LATE SUMMER

目錄

Late Summer

BRIGHT ORANGE SHAKE

材料

Yields 2 liters

2 mangos,
peeled and pitted

4 figs

1 cup mint leaves

1 lime, peeled

4 walnuts

1 Tbs.
coconut oil

6 ice cubes

2 cups water

Blend all ingredients in a heavy duty blender until fully combined and smooth. Serve immediately.

GOOD TO KNOW

To make hard cheese, substitute cashews with Macadamia nuts that have been dried in a food dehydrator at 41°C for 24 hours. The cheese will consolidate to a hard cheese texture.

Tri-color Cashew Cheese Rolls

Step 1

In a blender set at high speed, process ingredients into a fully incorporated mixture. Wrap in cheese cloth and place under a jar filled with water (this functions as a weight). Place in a colander set over a deep bowl and leave at room temperature for 24 hours until all the liquid is drained.

Step 2

Remove cheese from cloth, and process in a blender with lemon juice, salt and beer yeast. Divide cheese into 3 portions, placing each in a separate bowl. Add seasoning ingredients and mix. Place three 8 cm. aluminum rings on a flat plate. Transfer cheese mixtures to rings. Refrigerate for at least 12 hours.

材料

Yields 3 rolls

Step 1

2 cups cashews, soaked for 2 hours

1 cup water

1 tsp. acidophilus probiotic powder (available in health food stores and drugstores)

Step 2

3/4 tsp. salt

2 tsp. beer yeast

1-2 tsp. lemon juice

Cheese Seasonings

Red

1/4 red bell pepper, chopped

4 sun dried tomatoes

1 tsp. dried oregano

1/4 red onion

1 tsp. paprika or
1/4 tsp. chili powder

Yellow

1/4 yellow bell pepper, chopped

1 tsp. turmeric

1 tsp. dried thyme

1 clove garlic

Green

1 clove garlic, crushed

1/2 tsp. ground black or white pepper

1/4 cup dill, chopped

2 scallions, finely chopped

SPREADS

材料

Sun-dried Tomatoes, Walnut and Ginger Spread

Yields 250 gr.

1 cup sun-dried tomatoes

1 cup walnuts

1 tsp. coarse Atlantic sea salt

1/2 tsp. coarsely ground black pepper

2 cloves garlic

1 onion

1 Tbs. grated fresh ginger root

juice from 1/2 a lemon

1/2 cup olive oil

1/2 cup water at room temperature

Indian Pesto

Yields 250 gr.

1 bunch basil

1 bunch coriander

1/2 cup mint leaves

8 cloves garlic

1 cup olive oil

1 tsp. coarse Atlantic sea salt

1-2 fresh or dried chili pepper

1 tsp. lemon juice (optional)

Sprouted Black Lentil and Walnut Spread

Yields 250 gr.

1 cup black lentils, sprouted and cooked

5 sun-dried tomatoes

1/2 cup walnuts

1 cup parsley, chopped

2 Tbs. olive oil

1 tsp. cumin

1 tsp. coarse Atlantic sea salt

juice from 1 lemon

Process all ingredients in a food processor to desired consistency.

Joy Crackers

材料

Yields 500 gr.

100 gr. flax seeds

100 gr. sunflower seeds

100 gr. pumpkin seeds

100 gr. sesame seeds

100 gr. walnuts

1 fresh chili pepper

1/4 cup sun-dried tomatoes

1 tsp. coarse Atlantic sea salt

1 tsp. cumin

1 Tbs. olive oil

Soak all seeds for 2 hours. Squeeze out the liquid. In a food processor, combine seeds with the remaining ingredients and process for several minutes.

Thinly spread mixture on Teflex sheets. Dry in a food dehydrator at 40°C for 24 hours. If using a regular oven, preheat to 150°C. Line a baking pan with parchment paper. Using a spatula, thinly spread mixture onto paper. Bake for 30 minutes. Remove pan from oven, cut dough into squares using a sharp knife, return to oven and bake for 15 minutes. Turn crackers over and bake for an additional 15 minutes.

GOOD TO KNOW

These crispy, delicious crackers are an excellent addition to a gluten free diet or to help cleanse gluten from the body. Substitute spices with the seasoning of your choice. Flax seeds help cleanse the digestive system, and are particularly effective in relieving symptoms of Lazy Bowel Syndrome. When soaked for an hour or more, the seeds excrete a gummy substance that binds the ingredients together.

Puccini Zucchini

材料

Serves 8

6 zucchini

6 tomatoes

4 cloves garlic

1/4 cup
Kalamata olives

1 red onion

1/4 cup
sun-dried tomatoes

pinch chili pepper

1 cup fresh basil

3 sprigs fresh thyme

Using a vegetable peeler, slice zucchini into long thin strips (discard seeds). Process remaining ingredients in a food processor to a coarse consistency. Pour sauce over zucchini. Serve immediately.

GOOD TO KNOW

This is a fresh, chilled "raw food" dish. "Raw foods" retain the nutritional values of soluble fibers, vitamins and enzymes that are lost when heated to temperatures over 41°C. To serve this dish warm, I recommend heating the sauce over a low flame to desired temperature. This dish is an excellent substitute for wheat pasta. The zucchini can be replaced with carrots and cucumber or a combination of your choice.

Root Vegetables in Bamboo Steamer

材料

Serves 4

Bamboo Steamer

2 fennel

250 gr. pumpkin

2 sweet potatoes or carrots

2 small onions

2 kohlrabi

2 beets

1 round squash

To serve

1 Tbs. sesame seeds

1 tsp. coarse Atlantic sea salt

juice from 1/2 a lemon

1 tsp. ground black pepper

2 Tbs. tahini paste

Rinse vegetables and cut in half. Arrange in a bamboo steamer placed over a pot of boiling water. If a steamer is not available, use a vegetable or couscous steamer. Steam for 20 minutes or until vegetables are soft. Sprinkle with sesame seeds, pepper and coarse salt. Drizzle tahini and a few drops of lemon juice on top. Serve.

GOOD TO KNOW

Steamed vegetables are an easy, healthy snack or side dish that can be enjoyed year round by combining seasonal produce. Topped with tahini, this dish is a rich source of calcium and iron.

Zucchini Salad with Champignon Mushrooms and Radish

長夏安中

材料

Serves 4

2 zucchini

10 fresh Champignon mushrooms

2 celery stalks

5 basil leaves

1 radish

1/4 cup Hijiki, not soaked

Dressing

juice from 1/2 a lemon

1 tsp. mirin

1/2 tsp. black pepper

1/2 tsp. coarse Atlantic sea salt

1 Tbs. olive oil

Rinse vegetables thoroughly. Cut mushrooms, radish and zucchini into rounds and then in half. Chop celery stalks. Leave basil leaves whole. Place salad ingredients in a bowl. Mix dressing ingredients and pour over vegetables. Garnish with Hijiki.

GOOD TO KNOW

Hijiki is a salt water seaweed. It is rich in iron, iodine, calcium and anti-oxidants. For this salad, I use dried, flaky Hijiki. Hijiki can be soaked in water for 15 minutes, and added to a variety of cooked dishes and salads. Although changing after soaking, its taste is still delicious. I like both options.

STUFFED ROUND SQUASH

材料

Serves 4

4 round squash

10 Champignon mushrooms, chopped

1 cup Macadamia nuts

5 basil leaves

1 tsp. coarse Atlantic sea salt

1/2 tsp. chili oil

1 tsp. curry powder

2 Tbs. water or as needed

Preheat oven to 180°C. Slice off tops of squash, set aside. Using a teaspoon, scoop out and discard pulp. In a blender, process Macadamia nuts, basil and spices while adding water to reach desired consistency. Add to chopped mushrooms. Stuff squash with filling and cover with tops. Arrange squash on a baking pan lined with parchment paper or in an ovenproof dish. Bake for 30 minutes. Squash can also be baked in a food dehydrator at 41°C for 24 hours or more, as needed.

GOOD TO KNOW

Food enzymes are destroyed at temperatures over 41°C. Baking in a food dehydrator retains the enzymes nutritional values. I first became aware of the many benefits of using a food dehydrator through my interest in Raw Food nutrition (a dietary practice of eating uncooked, unprocessed foods only).

Sweet Potato Gnocchi with Grilled Pepper Sauce

材料

Serves 4

2 sweet potatoes

1 cup
spelt flour

2 tsp. coarse
Atlantic sea salt

1/2 tsp. black pepper

5 basil leaves, chopped

chives for garnish

3 liters water

Sauce

3 bell peppers

2 cloves garlic

1/2 tsp. coarse
Atlantic sea salt

7 Kalamata olives, pitted

Peel sweet potatoes. Bake in preheated oven 200°C for 30 minutes or untill soft. Mash while still hot, gradually add flour, basil, 1 tsp. salt and 1/2 tsp. black pepper. Mix to dough-like texture. Set aside for 15 minutes. Divide dough into tennis ball size portions. Shape portions into long "snakes". Cut snakes into 1 cm. thick rounds.

In a deep pot, boil 3 liters water with 1 tsp. salt. Drop gnocchi into water and cook for 3-5 minutes after floating to the surface.

Sauce

Roast bell peppers over flame or in the oven until skin is charred. Place in a nylon bag for 15 minutes. Remove and peel. Transfer to a food processor or blender, add Kalamata olives, salt and 2 cloves garlic. Process until smooth.

To Serve

Ladle sauce onto plate, arrange gnocchi on top and garnish with chives.

GOOD TO KNOW

There are many varieties of sweet potato. In Chinese medicine, the sweet potato is associated with "earth" due to its orange color and sweet taste. Its high fiber content helps maintain a healthy digestive system, and curbs cravings for sweets. This dish upgrades potato-based traditional gnocchi.

Chilled Orange Almond Cream Soup

材料

Serves 4

Almond Milk

1 cup almonds, soaked for 12 hours

1 cup water

Soup

4 celery stalks

1 finger (5-6 cm.) fresh ginger root

2 cloves garlic

1 tsp. fresh chili or chili oil

4 carrots

1 lemon

pinch black pepper

1/2 cup parsley leaves

Almond Milk

Process almonds and water in a blender. Transfer to cheese cloth. Wring over a bowl to extract almond milk.

Soup

In a juicer, juice carrots, celery, ginger and garlic to make a clear juice. Juice lemon using a hand juicer. Combine almond milk, vegetable juice, lemon juice and spices. Pour into soup bowls and garnish with parsley.

Milky Choco-Almond Shake

Pour almond milk into a shaker or heavy duty blender. Add remaining ingredients and process to a smooth, fully incorporated consistency. Serve chilled.

材料

Yields 2 cups

1/2 liter almond milk (recipe on page 110)

2 Tbs. cocoa powder (preferably from unroasted beans)

2 tsp. maple syrup

1 tsp. cinnamon

4 dates, pitted

8 ice cubes

GOOD TO KNOW

The unroasted cocoa bean is the natural form of chocolate. Due to its unique mineral content and nutritional properties, natural cocoa is considered one of nature's super-foods. Rich in anti-oxidants, magnesium, iron and calcium, unroasted cocoa beans boost alertness and sexual arousal, and improve concentration, memory and blood flow.

Won-Kwang-Sa Pie

材料

For 26 cm. pie dish

Dough

2 cups walnuts

1 Tbs. coconut oil

4 dates, pitted

1 cup sugarless berry jam

Filling

3 Granny Smith apples

3 Tbs. coconut oil

4 Tbs. maple syrup

2 tsp. cinnamon

Chop walnuts in a food processor. Add 1 Tbs. coconut oil to make a smooth dough. Press the dough evenly onto the bottom of a pie dish. Spread jam over dough.

Peel and core apples. Cut into halves. In a pan, sweat apples in coconut oil for 4-5 minutes. Add maple syrup and cinnamon, and mix gently. Continue to cook until liquids are absorbed. Arrange apples in a swirl pattern on top of the dough. Cover and refrigerate for 1 hour.

SEASONAL FRUIT ICE CREAM CONE

材料

Yields 8 cones

Cone

1 cup flax seed, ground into flour

1/2 cup cashews, ground into flour

1/2 cup spelt, finely ground into flour

3 Tbs. lemon juice

3 Tbs. date honey or maple syrup

1/2 tsp. coarse Atlantic sea salt

2 tsp. vanilla extract

1 pear, peeled and cored

1/2 cup water

1/2 cup almonds, coarsely ground

1/4 cup pistachios, coarsely ground

Cone

In food processor, process flours with all ingredients except almonds and pistachios. Transfer to a bowl, add almonds and pistachios, and combine into an elastic dough. Roll the dough into a 12 cm. diameter round and place on an oven grid lined with parchment paper or Teflex. Dry in the oven at 150°C for 15 minutes, or in a food dehydrator at 41°C for 4-5 hours.

Cut dough into rounds using a 12 cm. diameter ring. Roll into cones, securing bottoms with toothpicks. Oven dry on unlined oven grid for 15 minutes, or in a food hydrator for 4 hours until cones are crispy.

Seasonal Fruit Ice Cream Cone

長夏安中

材料

Ice cream

Yields 1 kg.

500 gr. seasonal fruit. (in late summer, I recommend using mango, melon, black plums or fresh figs).

1 cup coconut oil

500 gr. cashews, soaked for 12 hours

1 cup pistachios

1 cup almonds, soaked for 12 hours

1 cup mint leaves, rinsed

2 cups ice cubes

zest from 1 lemon

1 Tbs. ground ginger root

Blend all ingredients to a coarse consistency. Freeze for 2 hours. Fill cones with ice cream and serve.

I recommend using a heavy-duty blender.

GOOD TO KNOW

Making ice cream with your kids guarantees hours of quality time and fun with the extra benefit of teaching them how delicious ice cream can be without using milk, food coloring, artificial preservatives and gluten.

Truffles

材料

Yields 20

3/4 cup
almond butter

1/2 cup maple syrup
or rice malt

1/2 tsp. vanilla extract

1/3 cup cocoa powder

1/3 cup cocoa butter,
melted

pinch coarse
Atlantic sea salt

1/4 cup water

Optional toppings

finely ground coconut

ground pistachio nuts

cinnamon-cocoa
powder combination

In a blender, process all truffle ingredients to a fully incorporated and thick consistency. Refrigerate for at least 12 hours or until cream is hardened. Using an ice cream scoop, create large balls. Cut in half and form small identically sized balls. Gently roll in the coating of your choice. Keep refrigerated.

GOOD TO KNOW

This recipe is based on a recipe from the Matthew Kenny Academy of Oklahoma City. Promoting raw-super-vegan cuisine, the academy's restaurant is testimony to Kenny's conviction that vegans can savor the wonderful flavors nature has to offer.

HOMEMADE HEALING CHOCOLATE

材料

1 1/2 cups cocoa powder

1 1/2 cups coconut oil

1 cup maple syrup,
rice malt or date honey

**Optional Additions
(1 cup each)**

ground almonds

coarsely ground
pistachio nuts

Goji berries
(available dried at
health food stores)

cranberries

grated orange zest

grated lemon zest

cocoa shavings

coconut shavings

Mix dry and wet ingredients until fully incorporated. If coconut oil is consolidated, melt in a bain marie. Add additions of your choice.

Pour mixture into praline molds.

Note: Additions should be prepared in quantities of 1 cup each. If using more than one, combine to produce 1 cup. For instance: 1/4 cup ground pistachios, 1/4 cup cranberries and 1/2 cup cocoa shavings.

秋收

BE SILENT
SCATTERED AUTUMN SHOWERS
GOING OUT TO GATHER FOOD
TO COLLECT
SPRING WATER

ZEN MASTER RYOKAN

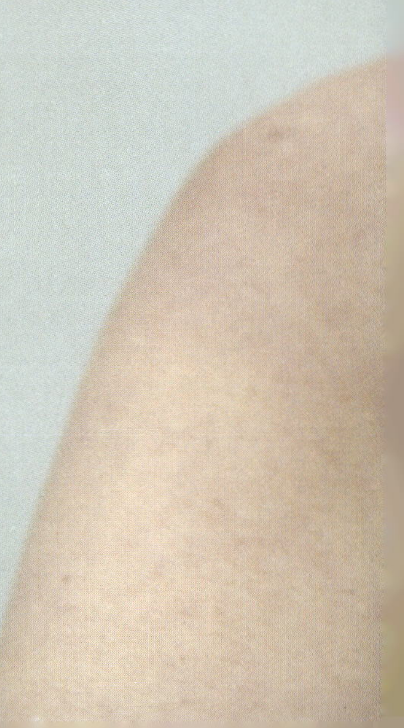

AUTUMN

目錄

AUTUMN

Vegetable and Tofu Antipasti

秋收

材料

Serves 4

1 eggplant

1 red bell pepper

500 gr. Jerusalem artichokes

1 sweet potato

1 kohlrabi

1 beet

1 turnip

2 heads garlic

100 gr. tofu

1 Tbs. soy sauce

Sauce

3 cloves garlic, crushed

1/4 cup olive oil

1 tsp. herb salt

Preheat oven to 180°C. Dice the tofu and marinate for 15 minutes in 2 Tbs. water and 1 Tbs. soy sauce. Rinse vegetables thoroughly and cut into 1 cm. thick slices. Rinse garlic heads and leave whole. Arrange vegetables and tofu on a baking pan lined with parchment paper. Mix all sauce ingredients in a separate bowl. Using a brush, coat vegetables generously with sauce and roast for 15 minutes. Turn vegetables over and roast for an additional 15 minutes.

GOOD TO KNOW

Herb salt adds that extra pizzzazz to a wide variety of dishes. It's easy to make – here's how: sun dry an assortment of fresh herbs such as thyme, oregano and rosemary. When dry, crush herbs using a mortar and pestle (your fingers will also do). Combine 1/2 cup of herbs with 1 cup coarse Atlantic sea salt. Bon appetite!

KING OYSTER ST. JACQUES IN LEMON SAUCE

材料

Serves 4

4 King Oyster mushrooms

1 tsp. sesame seeds

Marinade

1 Tbs. ginger root, grated

3 garlic cloves

1 Tbs. sesame oil

juice from 2 lemons

1 Tbs. soy sauce

Garnish

1 tsp. Hijiki

Slice mushrooms into 1/2 cm. rounds. Mix marinade ingredients and marinate mushrooms for 1 hour. Drain and arrange mushrooms on food dehydrator pan (save marinade). Dry at 41°C for 6 hours. Alternatively, arrange mushrooms on a cookie sheet and bake in the oven at 150°C for 30 minutes.

To serve: drizzle 1 tsp. marinade over mushrooms, sprinkle with sesame seeds and garnish with a strand of Hijiki.

GOOD TO KNOW

This is a vegetarian version of scallops in a creamy butter and wine sauce. Originating in China, the King Oyster mushroom is rich in anti-oxidants. Known for its unique flavor and meaty texture, this low calorie mushroom is a perfect sea-food substitute.

Creamy Black Lentil Soup

GOOD TO KNOW

Lentils are a popular staple in India where they are served with Basmati rice.

Soak lentils for 8 hours. Drain and sprout for 1 day, rinsing at least twice. Grate tomato, garlic and ginger. Combine with spices in a small bowl, transfer to a medium size pot and sweat lightly in olive oil. Add lentils and water. Bring to the boil. Lower heat and simmer for 2 hours or until lentils are soft. If you like your soup extra smooth, blend with a hand blender.

材料

Serves 8

500 gr. small (beluga) black lentils

6 garlic cloves

1 tomato

1 finger (6 cm.) ginger root

1 tsp. ground cumin

1 tsp. black pepper

2 tsp. curry powder

1 tsp. course Atlantic sea salt

1 Tbs. olive oil

4 liters water (to cover ingredients)

Traditional Moroccan Couscous

材料

Serves 6

Soup

100 gr. dried chickpeas

250 gr. pumpkin

1 zucchini

3 carrots

1 parsley root

1 celery root

5 celery stalks

1/2 cauliflower

1/4 green cabbage

1 turnip

1 leek

2 garlic cloves

1 onion

1/2 cup coriander leaves, chopped

1/2 cup parsley leaves, chopped

2 tsp. Baharat (Middle Eastern spice mix)

2 tsp. turmeric

1 tsp. ground black pepper

2 Tbs. course Atlantic sea salt

8 cups water

Soup

Place chickpeas in a large bowl and cover with cold tap water. Soak for a minimum of 8 hours. Make sure to change the water twice. Rinse and sprout for 24 hours. Place chickpeas in a pressure cooker or large pot. Cook for 1 1/2 hours or until chickpeas are soft but not mushy. Rinse the vegetables, cut into large pieces and place in the bottom of a couscous pot. Add just enough water to cover the vegetables. Add spices and chickpeas and bring to the boil. Lower heat and simmer for 1 hour and 20 minutes. In the meantime, soak coriander and parsley in water for 15 minutes. Add to soup and cook for an additional 10 minutes. For kids who might prefer soup without leaves, tie parsley and coriander with string, place in soup and remove before serving.

Traditional Steamed Couscous

Combine all couscous ingredients in a bowl, cover with water and let stand for 5 minutes. Transfer to top part (colander) of couscous pot. Gently rub couscous between the palms of your hands to separate lumps. Steam over soup on low heat for 20 minutes. If not serving immediately, remove colander and cover with a small towel.

Traditional Service: place 4 Tbs. couscous in a soup bowl. Add 3-4 Tbs. vegetables and chickpeas (without liquid). Add approximately 1/2 cup soup to lightly saturate couscous.

GOOD TO KNOW

Traditional Moroccan couscous is made with white, ground and processed semolina. In my mother's house, couscous meals marked the coming of autumn and the beginning of the Jewish New Year. Some of the ingredients in this recipe are substituted with healthier options: the processed semolina is replaced with more nutritious whole grain semolina. Semolina bran contains soluble fibers that cleanse the digestive system; its sprouts contain vitamin E that protect the skin against the hazards free radicals.

材料

Couscous

1 package whole grain couscous (100 gr.)

1 Tbs. olive oil

1 tsp. salt

2 cups boiling water

1/4 tsp. turmeric

COLORFUL PAELLA WITH FRESH SHITAKE MUSHROOMS

Preheat oven to 180°C. Dice tofu and mushrooms, and marinate in soy sauce, ginger and curry for 1 hour. Soak rice in tap water for 30 minutes, drain and leave to dry in colander. Roast saffron threads in the paella pot for 3 minutes. Remove and set aside in a small bowl. Add leeks and garlic to pot and sauté in olive oil until lightly browned. Add rice, vegetables, spices and saffron threads. Mix and add broth or water. Bring to the boil, lower the heat and simmer for 7 minutes. Place in oven and bake for 20 minutes. Add tofu and mushrooms and bake for an additional 10 minutes.

Garnish with chopped cilantro and serve.

材料

Serves 4

Large Dutch Oven or oven-proof pot with fitted lid

500 gr. whole Basmati rice

2 leeks, sliced into rounds

2 celery stalks, chopped

1/2 package Hijiki, soaked in water

4 garlic cloves, chopped

1 red bell pepper, diced into small cubes

1 large tomato, peeled and diced

100 gr. tofu

10 fresh Shitake mushrooms

4 King Oyster mushrooms

2 tsp. olive oil

1 Tbs. course Atlantic sea salt

2 Tbs. soy sauce

1/2 tsp. curry powder

2 Tbs. grated ginger root

1/2 tsp. chili powder

1 tsp. ground black pepper

20 saffron threads, soaked in 1/4 cup hot water

3 cups vegetable broth or water

1 cup chopped cilantro

GOOD TO KNOW

This recipe is quick, healthy and wholesome "fast food". Substitute ingredients with whatever's in season or with whatever's available in your fridge. Delicious both hot and cold.

Stir Fried Tofu with Seasonal Green Beans

Soak Hijiki in cold water for 15 minutes, rinse and drain. In a heated wok, stir fry tofu, 1 Tbs. oil, salt and curry until tofu is golden. Set aside. Sauté onions in 1 Tbs. oil until golden. Add garlic and sauté for 2-3 minutes. Add green beans and stir fry for a few minutes longer. Add mushrooms and stir fry for 3-4 minutes. Add tofu and Hijiki, mix and sprinkle with sesame seeds.

材料

Serves 4

1 package (200 gr.) tofu, cubed

1/2 cup Hijiki

1 1/2 onions, sliced into strips

500 gr. fresh green beans, trimmed and halved

4 Shitake mushrooms, quartered

2 King Oyster mushrooms, quartered

1 Portobello mushroom, quartered

1 tsp. fresh grated ginger root

1 tsp. curry powder

1/2 tsp. course Atlantic sea salt

1/4 cup black or white sesame seeds

2 Tbs. olive or sesame oil

2 cloves garlic, grated

2 Tbs. soy sauce

While working on this book, I lost several dear friends and family members who accompanied me on my journey and played significant roles in my life.

One of them was my father, Gaby Sebbag, whose passing made me realize how blessed I was to have matured by his side, and the true meaning of loss.

An ending and a beginning, a beginning and an end, and so forth.

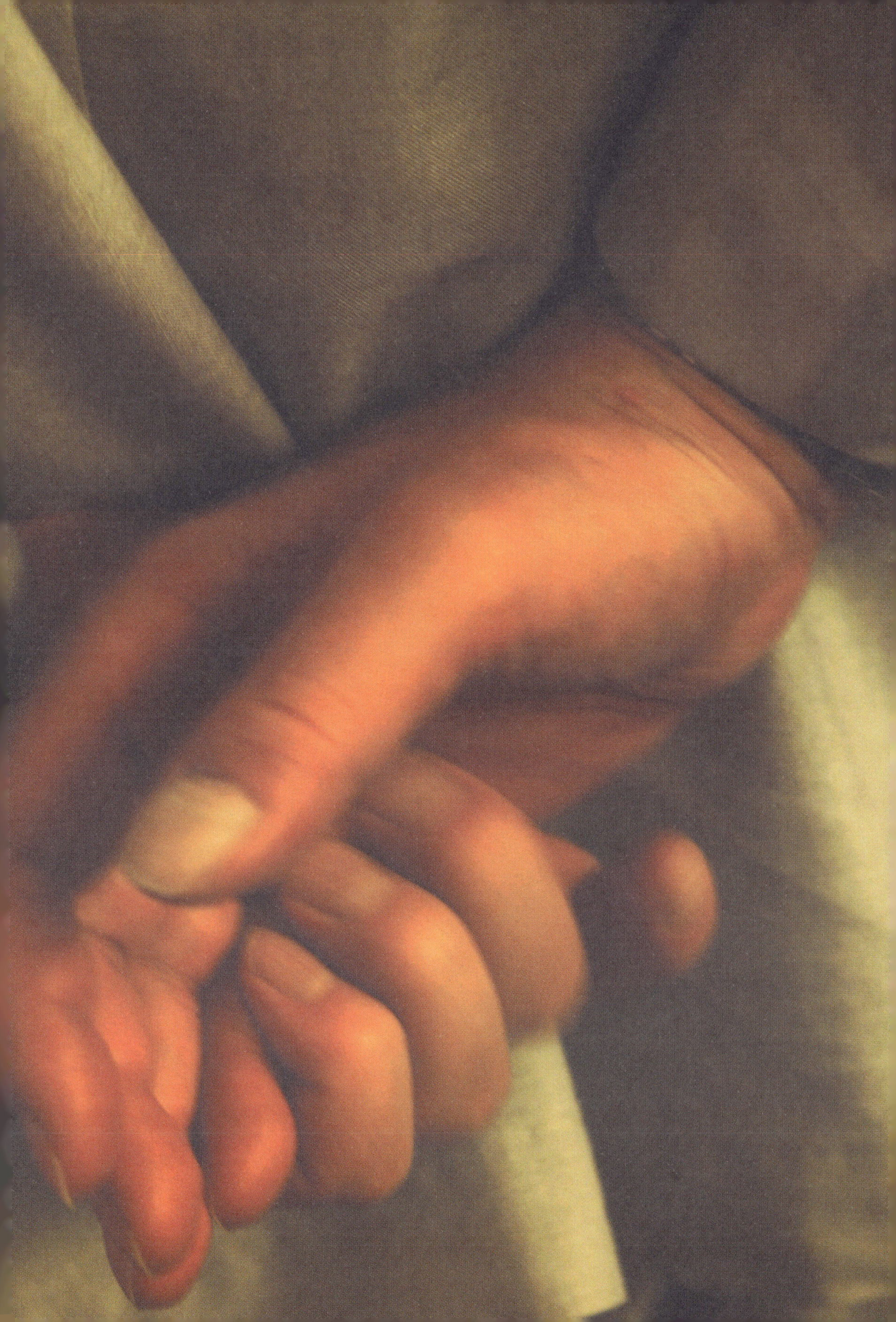

HEARTY ROOT SOUP

材料

Serves 6

1 large onion

1 parsley root

10 Champignon mushrooms

2 fennel

2 cups cauliflower, cut into florets

1 celery root, including stalks

3 cloves garlic

2 cups chopped coriander

2 cups chopped parsley

1 tsp. coarse Atlantic sea salt

1 tsp. caraway seeds

1 Tbs. grated ginger root

1 whole chili pepper

3 liters water

Rinse all thoroughly, and cut into large cubes. Place vegetables in a large pot, add spices and water to cover. Bring to the boil, lower heat and simmer for 1 1/2 hours. Puree in a blender or in the pot using a hand blender. Divide into soup bowls, drizzle with 2 drops olive oil and a drop of lemon juice.

GOOD TO KNOW

Hot spices help strengthen the lungs. Using them in autumn boosts the immune system and prepares the body for winter – a natural immunization shot!

Three Variations on Tofu Kebabs

材料

Yields 6 skewers

300 gr. tofu

1 red bell pepper

6 shallots, halved

1 zucchini

Cut tofu into 2 cm. cubes (approx. 24 cubes), and divide into three equal portions. In three separate bowls, combine ingredients for each marinade. Marinate tofu portions for 1 hour. Cut zucchini into 2 cm. thick rounds. Cut red pepper into equally sized squares. Push skewers through tofu cubes and vegetables. Grill on BBQ or grill pan. Turn until lightly browned on all sides.

Mediterranean marinade

1 tsp. paprika (sweet or hot)

1 tsp. cumin

1 clove garlic

2 Tbs. olive oil

Japanese marinade

2 Tbs. soy sauce

1 tsp. rice malt

1 Tbs. sesame oil

1 clove garlic

Indian marinade

1 tsp. curry powder

1 tsp. tandoori paste

1 tsp. chili oil

2 Tbs. olive oil

1/2 tsp. coarse Atlantic sea salt

Pomacello Aperitif

材料

Serves 4

4 pomegranates

16 ice cubes

1 Tbs. date honey, maple syrup or molasses

1 tsp. grated ginger root

juice from 1 lemon

GOOD TO KNOW

In Jewish tradition the pomegranate symbolizes blessings, wealth, beauty and wisdom. Its many properties include anti-oxidants, iron and a variety of vitamins and minerals that help decrease blood pressure and cholesterol as well as inhibiting various types of cancer. Pomegranate seeds are a great addition to salads; its juice makes a healthy, thirst-quenching drink.

In a blender, crush ice with date honey, ginger and lemon juice. Juice pomegranates using an electric or hand press juicer. Combine pomegranate juice with ice mixture. Pour into glasses and garnish with pomegranate seeds.

Açai Sorbet

GOOD TO KNOW

Açai is cultivated in Brazil. It is considered a super anti-oxidant, and a rare source of Vitamin E. Açai is rich in iron, fatty acids and calcium.

材料

Yields 2-3 cups

200 gr. frozen Açai

2 ripe mangos

3 Tbs. date honey

1 banana

10 ice cubes

1 lime, peeled

Combine all ingredients in a blender. Blend until smooth. Serve immediately.

Eggplant and Zucchini Rolls

材料

Yields 22 rolls

1 zucchini

1 eggplant

22 basil leaves, rinsed

1/2 cup Macadamia nut cheese (recipe on page 170)

Cut zucchini and eggplant into thin slices. Arrange on a roasting pan and roast in the oven, or sear on a lightly oiled heavy pan over a high flame. Cool. Place 1 tsp. Macadamia nut cheese in the center of each slice and top with a basil leaf. Roll.

Cauliflower and Pumpkin in Macadamia Nut Cheese

Preheat oven to 180°C. Rinse cauliflower and pumpkin thoroughly. Soak cauliflower in salted water for 15 minutes. Divide into florets. Cut pumpkin into 1/2 cm. wedges and arrange on a baking pan lined with parchment paper. Process cream ingredients with 1/2 cup water in a heavy duty blender. Gradually add water until you've reached the desired consistency. Using a spatula, spread cream on cauliflower and pumpkin. Bake for 45 minutes.

材料

Serves 4

1 cauliflower

250 gr. pumpkin

1 Tbs. coarse Atlantic sea salt

Cream

1 cup Macadamia nuts, soaked for 12 hours

1 cup cashews, soaked for 12 hours

1/2 cup water

1 shallot

2 cloves garlic

1 Tbs. white miso

1/2 tsp. turmeric

juice from 1/2 a lemon

BITE-SIZE BEET AND ZUCCHINI ROLLS

材料

Yields 10

1 beet

1 zucchini

1 carrot

1 cucumber

4 scallions

10 chives

1 cup sunflower sprouts

1 cup mung bean sprouts

Pesto sauce for zucchini (recipe on page 98)

Asian dressing for beets (recipe on page 73)

To save time, I recommend using a mandolin slicer for this recipe.

Rinse vegetables and pat dry. Slice beets into 1 mm. thick wedges. Slice zucchini into 3 mm. thick rounds. Julienne carrot, cucumber and scallions. Place 1 tsp. pesto on the top edge of each zucchini slice. Stack 3 carrot juliennes, 3 cucumber juliennes, a small bunch each of sunflower and mash bean sprouts and a slice of scallion. Roll and tie with 2 chives. Repeat with beets and Asian sauce.

GOOD TO KNOW

This dish is the star of cocktail catering, and a perfect "raw food" appetizer. Its fresh and colorful ingredients provide a unique opportunity to savor the wholesome flavors of vegetables that are usually not consumed raw, such as beets and zucchini.

冬藏

HOT STEW
AND THE SCENT OF SPICES
FILL
THE HOUSE
WARM
AND OUTSIDE IT IS COLD.

AVITAL SEBBAG

WINTER

目錄

WINTER

GOOD TO KNOW

Limes and lemons have extraordinary antiseptic qualities. That's why I keep them in my kitchen all year round. Although sour, lemons and limes are a basic staple, recommended as wonderful accompaniments to watermelon, grapefruit and mango. The color and subtle flavors of citrus fruit and honey remind me of that are usually not consumed raw, such as beets and zucchini. rays of winter's sun.

Sunny Winter Drink

Peel oranges and lime, and cut into large cubes. Rinse apples and ginger (do not peel). Place all ingredients in a heavy duty blender. Add water and blend until smooth and fully combined.

材料

Yields 2 liters

4 oranges

4 limes

4 Granny Smith apples

2-3 cm. ginger root

1 Tbs. coconut oil

2 Tbs. date honey

1/2 cup water

Yellow Lentil Soup with a Twist

材料

Serves 8

500 gr.
yellow lentils

1 onion

2 leeks

2 yellow
bell peppers

1 medium
cauliflower

2 fennel

1 Tbs. olive oil

1 tsp. turmeric

1 tsp. caraway seeds

1 fresh
red chili pepper
or 1 tsp. chili oil

pinch
"4 seasons" pepper

1 Tbs. coarse
Atlantic sea salt

5 liters water

Garnish

1 package
mung bean sprouts

juice from 1 lemon

1 Tbs. ground hyssop

Soak lentils overnight. Rinse until water runs clear. Rinse all vegetables thoroughly and dice. Stir-fry vegetables in a soup pot with olive oil for a few minutes. Add spices and stir-fry for 2-3 minutes. Add lentils and water. Bring to the boil. Reduce heat and cook for 30 minutes. Using a hand blender or food processor, blend until smooth and fully combined. Garnish with sprouts, hyssop and a drop of lemon juice.

GOOD TO KNOW

This cauliflower, fennel and lentil combination is surprisingly unique. The soup's yellow color compliments its hearty, warm flavors. The spicy chili pepper enhances the blood flow and warms the body on cold winter days.

Korean Miso Soup

材料

Serves 10

2 parsley roots

2 celery roots

6 celery stalks, chopped

6 carrots

2 onions

6 liters water

1/2 cup Wakame or Kombu seaweed

8 Shitake mushrooms

5 cloves garlic

1 package (250 gr.) mung bean sprouts

1 cup dark brown, organic miso

200 gr. tofu, cubed

Rinse all vegetables thoroughly. Soak seaweed and Shitake mushrooms in lukewarm water for 15 minutes. Rinse thoroughly. Quarter onions and slice carrots into thin rounds. Cut celery and parsley roots into 2 cm. slices. Place vegetables and water in a large pot, bring to the boil, reduce heat and cook for 30 minutes.

Before serving: mix miso with 1 cup cold water and add to pot. Place 1/4 cup tofu cubes and sprouts in soup bowls, add soup and serve.

GOOD TO KNOW

Miso ("Chiang" in Chinese) is made from soy beans and is prepared in most Korean households. Its origin is most probably in China where it was a staple in vegetarian Buddhist cuisine. Prepared through a fermentation process that enhances its nutritional value with bacteria vital for the digestive system, miso is considered the healthiest of soy-based foods. In one of the South Korean monasteries I visited, a large clay pot containing 10 year old miso stood in the center of the kitchen. White miso can be used to season salads or as a spread.

Healthy Winter Sandwich

材料

Yields 4

1 avocado, peeled

8 slices sour dough bread (recipe on page 50)

4 tsp. Indian Pesto (recipe on page 98)

1/4 cup broccoli sprouts

2 pickles in brine

4 arugula (rocket) leaves

2 Champignon mushrooms

1 carrot

4 Tbs. tahini paste

1/2 cup dill

Rinse and dry vegetables. Slice carrot into thin strips using a peeler. Cut mushrooms and pickles into thin slices. Cut avocado into strips. Chop dill and arugula. Assemble sandwiches: spread 4 slices of bread with tahini paste and the spread of your choice. Stack avocado, carrots, mushrooms and pickles, top with sprouts, dill and arugula. Close each sandwich with a slice of bread.

冬藏

Tricolor Seaweed and Vegetable Winter Salad

材料

Soak seaweed in water for 15 minutes, rinse and drain. Rinse cucumber and carrot, discard ends and grate using a coarse grater, food processor fitted with grater or julienne peeler. Rinse and chop spinach and mint leaves. Place in a salad bowl. Add Wakame and remaining vegetables. In a food processor, process all dressing ingredients to a smooth, fully combined consistency. Pour over salad and sprinkle with sesame seeds.

Serves 4

1 cup Hijiki

1 cup Wakame

1 cucumber

1 carrot

1 cup spinach

1/4 cup mint leaves

1 Tbs. white or black sesame seeds

Dressing

2 cloves garlic

2 Tbs. soy sauce

juice from 2 lemons

juice from 1 tangerine or orange

1/4 ginger root, grated

1/2 tsp. chili pepper

Stir-fried Mushrooms, Bok choy and Endive on a Bed of Bulgur

材料

Serves 4

4 Shitake mushrooms

4 King Oyster mushrooms

4 Champignon mushrooms

4 bok choy leaves (substitute with Swiss chard or spinach)

4 scallions

4 endive leaves

4 sun-dried tomatoes

1 Tbs. soy sauce

1 Tbs. grated fresh ginger root

1 clove garlic

1 tsp. coarse Atlantic sea salt

1 tsp. ground black pepper

2 cups coarse bulgur

Soak bulgur in 2 cups water for 1 hour. Rinse and drain. Rinse all vegetables thoroughly. Stem mushrooms and cut into thin slices. Chop remaining vegetables. In a wok, stir-fry mushrooms in olive oil for 10 minutes. Add vegetables and spices. Stir-fry for 5 minutes. Serve over a bed of bulgur.

GOOD TO KNOW

King Oyster and Shitake mushrooms are staples in vegan cookery. Their meaty texture make them excellent fish substitutes. Due to their anti-cancer benefits, these mushrooms are widely used in Chinese medicine herb formulas.

GOOD TO KNOW

Vegan sushi can be prepared without rice. Using the traditional technique, place a leaf of Butterhead lettuce on Nori, add vegetables, and roll. This is a great recipe for those of us who have trouble digesting whole rice.

Gimbap – Korean Sushi

材料

Yields 4 rolls

4 Nori sheet

2 cups whole short grained rice, cooked and chilled

1 tsp. sesame oil

1 tsp. soy sauce

1 tsp. sesame seeds

Umeboshi sauce, or Dijon mustard

1 scallion, julienned

1 cucumber, julienned

1 carrot, julienned

1/2 cup sunflower sprouts

1 avocado, cut into thin strips

50 gr. tofu, cut into strips, marinated in soy sauce, and steamed in the oven

fresh Shitake mushrooms, marinated in soy sauce, and steamed in the oven

1 red bell pepper, thinly sliced (optional)

Butterhead lettuce

pistachios and sunflower seeds

To serve

Wasabi

soy sauce

Rice preparation

Soak rice for 1 day. Drain and cover with water in a large pot. Bring to the boil, reduce heat and cook covered until the water is absorbed, approximately 40 minutes. Transfer rice to a bowl (preferably wooden). Add 1 tsp. each sesame oil and sesame seeds. Mix well.

Sushi Rolls

Place bamboo sushi mat on a clean surface. Place 1 Nori sheet on the mat, coarse side up. Using a wooden spoon, spread rice on the top half of the leaf, approximately 1/2 cm. thick. Arrange vegetables on the bottom quarter of the leaf. Top with lettuce to cover vegetables and approximately 1/3 third of the leaf. Sprinkle with pistachios and sunflower seeds. Dampen top edge of leaf. To roll: lift the sushi mat at the edge closest to you, roll half way. Next, separate mat from Nori, and roll once. Rotate mat so that exposed Nori is closest to you. Finally, press mat onto the entire length of the Nori. Remove roll from mat.

To serve

Using a sharp knife, cut roll in half. Cut each half in two, or into desired width. Serve with Wasabi and soy sauce.

Stuffed Mushrooms with Macadamia Nut Cheese

材料

Serves 4

12 large Champignon or King Oyster mushrooms

Macadamia Nut Cheese

2 cups Macadamia nuts

6 sun-dried tomatoes

1/2 cup basil leaves

4 cloves garlic

1/4 cup olive oil

1 tsp. coarse Atlantic sea salt

pinch ground black pepper

GOOD TO KNOW

Professional chefs use paper towel to clean mushrooms without damaging their natural form and color. Originally, I prepared this recipe using goat cheese. Due to their meaty texture and 65% vegetable oil content, I often use ground macadamia nuts as a substitute for flour, dairy products and oil. Macadamia nuts are a recommended source of potassium and calcium.

Preheat oven to 180°C. Gently rinse mushrooms in cold water. Discard stems, leaving a cavity for stuffing. Process nuts and remaining ingredients in a food processor until creamy. Stuff mushrooms and arrange on a baking pan lined with parchment paper. Bake for 20 minutes.

Mom's Homemade Chickpea Stew

材料

Serves 4

500 gr. small
dried chickpeas

1 large onion

6 cloves garlic

6 tomatoes

1 tsp. coarsely
ground black pepper

1 tsp. turmeric
(or 1 tsp. grated
fresh turmeric root)

1 1/2 tsp. cumin

1 Tbs. coarse
Atlantic sea salt

To serve

whole rice,
whole couscous,
cooked bulgur
or barley

Soak chickpeas. Rinse and drain. To sprout, rinse and drain 3 times throughout the day.

Cook chickpeas in 3 liters water for 2 hours, or in a pressure cooker with 1 liter water for 1/2 hour. Drain. Reserve liquid.

Peel onion, chop and stir-fry with 1 Tbs. olive oil until golden. Rinse tomatoes and dice. Add to onions and sauté for 2 minutes. Add chickpeas, Spices and 4 cups reserved liquid. Bring to the boil, reduce heat and simmer, partially covered, for 1 1/2 hours. Serve on a bed of whole rice, whole couscous, bulgur or barley. For a perfect meal, serve with a spelt roll.

GOOD TO KNOW

One of my favorite childhood dishes, this stew is still a winner with family and friends. The combination of tomatoes, chickpeas and turmeric – a staple in Moroccan cooking – has a unique flavor, and is a rich source of essential proteins. According to philosopher Albertus Magnus, chickpeas have therapeutic attributes that enhance sperm count and quality, as well as increasing breast milk.

Spelt Rolls

In a mixing bowl, combine olive oil and maple syrup. Gradually add flour, oats, yeast and salt (if using an electric mixer, fit with a dough hook). Add water and knead for 10 minutes until dough is soft but not sticky. Cover bowl with a damp towel or plastic bag and keep in a warm place for 1 1/2 hours or 6 hours if using starter until dough is doubled in size. Transfer dough to a floured surface and divide into 25 balls. Knead each ball. Place balls on a baking sheet lined with parchment paper. Let rise for 30 minutes. Heat oven to 190°C. Sprinkle rolls with sesame seeds and salt. Bake for 20 minutes.

材料

Yields 25

1 kg. spelt flour

500 gr. sifted all-purpose flour

1 cup rolled oats

1 cup olive oil

1 Tbs. dry yeast or 1 cup sourdough starter

1 tsp. maple syrup

4-5 cups lukewarm water

1 Tbs. coarse Atlantic sea salt

Garnish

black sesame seeds

coarse Atlantic sea salt

Root Vegetable and Tofu Stew

材料

Serves 2

2 leeks

50 gr. yellow lentils

2 cloves garlic

50 gr. tofu

1 kohlrabi

2 celery stalks

1 fennel

1 sweet potato

4 Portobello mushrooms

1 beet root

1 fresh chili peppers

1/2 Tbs. turmeric

2 tsp. coarsely ground black pepper

2 Tbs. soy sauce

100cc boiling water

Preheat oven to 200°C. Dice tofu and mix with soy sauce. Marinate for 1/2 hour. Rinse vegetables thoroughly; do not peel. Cut vegetables into 2 cm. cubes. Arrange tofu and vegetables in individual clay or iron cauldrons. Mix spices in boiling water and pour over vegetables. Bake for 40 minutes.

GOOD TO KNOW

The Jerusalem artichoke is also known as sunroot. A staple in my mother's kitchen, this dish was my father's favorite. The recipe originated in Morocco where it is prepared with Cassava arrowroot and beef.

GOOD TO KNOW

Korean cuisine features dozens of Kimchi varieties all of which contain chili. Kimchi is a traditional Korean dish, served with every meal. It is prepared in what Koreans call a "container" – a black clay kettle – commonly found in all Korean kitchens. Vegetable pickling, or fermentation, is a process in which "good" bacteria (lactobacillus) is released from the vegetables in an acidic environment. Due to this process, the vegetables' shelf life is significantly prolonged while maintaining their taste and nutrients (vitamins, minerals, enzymes and phytochemicals).

Pickled Vegetables – Korean Kimchi in a Pickling Kettle

Cut cabbage into medium size pieces. Cut carrots and celery stalks on the angle into thin strips. Clean celery root and cut into medium size slices. Divide cauliflower into florets. Place all vegetables in a large bowl, add herbs, spices and water. Mix and transfer mixture to large, glass jars or a pickling kettle (sealed clay kettle, designed for pickling). Mark the preparation date on an adhesive label, and label jars or kettle. Place in a warm space (preferably in sunlight) for 3 days. Transfer to a shaded area for an additional 10 days.

材料

1 Chinese cabbage

1 cauliflower

4 celery roots

4 carrots

1 head celery

1 bunch fresh thyme

1 bunch oregano

i bunch tarragon

1 Tbs. "four seasons" pepper corns

8 Tbs. Atlantic sea coarse salt

10 cloves garlic

4 Tbs. Korean chili, hot paprika or chili pepper

5 bay leaves

4 liters water

GOOD TO KNOW

Tempeh is produced from fermented soy beans, making it one of the healthiest soy-based foods. To enhance its nutritional value, I recommend combining tempeh with a fresh vegetable or raw sprouts.

Stir-fried Tempeh with Jerusalem Artichokes

材料

Serves 4

1 package tempeh, diced

200 gr. pumpkin, peeled and diced

4 Swiss chard leaves, rinsed

4 Jerusalem artichokes, peeled and diced

1 package sunflower sprouts

1 tsp. curry powder

1 Tbs. olive oil

1 Tbs. soy sauce

1 tsp. chili oil

1/2 lemon

In a wok, stir-fry tempeh with olive oil and curry until browned. Add Jerusalem artichokes and stir-fry until soft. Add pumpkin and stir-fry for 7 minutes, until slightly softened. Cut Swiss chard into medium sized strips, add to wok and stir-fry for 2 minutes. Remove from heat, add sprouts, soy sauce and chili oil. Splash with lemon juice, toss and serve.

Bean, Lentil and Mushroom "Mesabaha"

材料

Serves 4

1/2 cup white kidney beans (or any variety of white beans)

2 cups yellow lentils

1 tsp. turmeric

1 tsp. cumin

5 Shitake mushrooms

15 assorted mushrooms

1 onion

2 Tbs. soy sauce

1/2 tsp. black ground pepper

3 cloves garlic

1/2 chili pepper (optional)

1/4 cup dry red wine

juice from 2 limes or lemons

2 Tbs. coarse Atlantic sea salt

1/4 cup chopped peanuts

1/2 cup olive oil

Soak beans in water for 10 hours. Drain and transfer to colander to sprout for 24 hours, rinsing every 8 hours. Cook beans in a pressure cooker with 1 Tbs. salt and 3 cloves garlic for 1 1/2 hours, or in a regular pot for 3-4 hours on low heat until soft. Drain and grind to a coarse consistency in a food processor.

Rinse lentils and cook in 4 cups water seasoned with turmeric and cumin until water evaporates and lentils soften into a thick puree.

Chop onion and sauté in a wok with 2 Tbs. olive oil until lightly browned. Rinse mushrooms, chop and add to onion. Stir-fry until mushrooms are soft. Add soy sauce, black pepper and wine, and cook for 5-6 minutes.

Spread bean spread on serving dish, top with lentil spread and mushrooms. Sprinkle with chopped peanuts, drizzle with olive oil and lemon juice and serve.

This recipe was inspired by Chef Erez Komorovsky's hot bean spread served during a workshop held on a cold winter's day at his home in the Galilee. A variation on traditional "mesabaha" made with chickpeas, this combination of warm colors and deep flavors nurtures both body and soul. A particularly rich source of protein, this recipe is a welcome addition to vegan cookery.

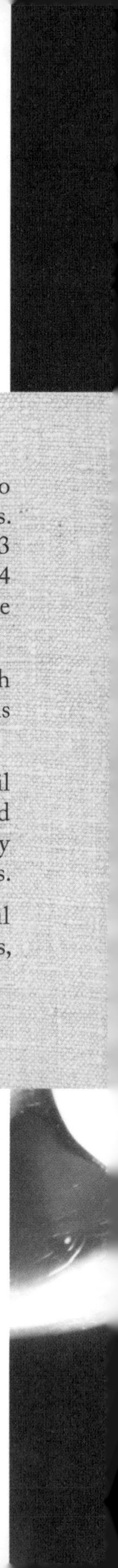

Rolled Oats Porridge

材料

Serves 4

16 Tbs. rolled oats

2 cups water

2 cups vanilla
flavored rice milk,
almond milk,
or oat milk

4 Tbs. "cereal mix"
(see recipe below)

4 tsp. sweetener
(date honey,
molasses or
maple syrup)

Optional

1/2 cup
diced seasonal fruit

Cereal Mix

Yields 1 liter

2 cups assorted dried fruit,
diced into small cubes

2 cups ground almonds,
walnuts and coconut

4 tsp. cinnamon

Cook oats, water, your choice of milk and sweetener for 15 minutes to desired consistency. Adding liquids and cooking for longer will yield a smooth, thinner porridge. Pour porridge into bowls, add cereal mix.

GOOD TO KNOW

Porridge is a staple food in the Far East. Highly nutritious, satisfying and economical, porridge is the conventional breakfast food in Zen monasteries.

Spice Cake

材料

24 cm. cake pan, or loaf pan

1 cup coconut oil

2 cups apple juice

1/2 cup date honey

2 cups spelt flour

1 Tbs. baking powder

1 cup raisins

1 cup pecans, finely ground

1 tsp. cinnamon

1 tsp. vanilla extract

4 bananas, mashed

zest from 1 lemon

1/2 cup ground cocoa beans

Preheat oven to 180°C. Mix all dry ingredients. in a mixing bowl. Gradually add liquid ingredients and beat until fully combined. Pour into baking pan. Bake for 1 1/2 hour.

冬藏

STRAWBERRY SORBET

Place all ingredients in a blender. Blend until smooth and fully combined. Pour into silicon cube mold. Freeze. To serve: garnish with chocolate shavings and thin date slices.

材料

Yields 24 cubes

30 strawberries

1 Tbs. coconut oil

1 Tbs. organic maple syrup

Mindful Eating

Mindful eating is a conscious, delicate and calm approach to eating. It involves developing awareness of the nutrients available to us in the foods we eat, while acknowledging breathing, chewing and swallowing as integral parts of the eating experience. Mindful eating means respecting the needs of both body and soul, and devoting time to satisfy these needs. In harmony with what nature provides throughout the five seasons, eating mindfully engages the five senses: sight, smell, touch, sound and taste. Mindfulness cultivates our ability to make choices that are right for us, that help us feel healthier, more energetic, vital and happy. By being aware of what and how we eat, we are likely to eat less and better digest our food. As a result, our body weight is balanced, and we may even lose those extra pounds. But more importantly, we feel energized, focused and attuned to our inner wisdom.

Basic Rules for Mindful Eating

Chewing: to fully enjoy the foods we eat and digest them properly, we begin by responding to the various tastes and textures in our mouth as we chew. Chewing each bite approximately 40 times optimizes vitamin and mineral absorption and digestion.

Drinking: to avoid diluting digestive juices in the stomach, avoid drinking during and for 30 minutes following meals. A glass of quality wine, on the other hand, is a welcome accompaniment to any meal.

Fruit: eat a fruit approximately half an hour before, or one hour after, meals containing protein. The combination of fruit and protein induces fermentation in the digestive track.

Moderation: eat in moderation and only when you feel hungry. Try and consume one main meal a day.

Eating before bedtime: make every effort to stop eating four hours before going to bed for the night.

Variation: experiment with new and exciting recipes based on seasonal ingredients.

Bowel movements: bowel movements should be daily and regular, painless and without irregular odors.

Quality meal time: try and talk as little as possible during meals, do not answer the phone or engage in other activities. Devote quiet, calm time to eating; engage all of your senses and enjoy your food to the max!

The joy of preparation: any successful meal begins with the joy of creating it. While cooking, concentrate on what you are doing, be calm, relaxed and as cheerful as possible. Feel like artists in the kitchen, be excited, experiment with new ingredients and recipes, and most importantly, always season your meals with an abundance of love.

Juice cleanse: juice fasts or cleansings are the best way to cleanse your system. Twice a year, nurture your body with green shakes and clear fruit juices for three days. This is the best way to rest body, mind and soul.

For more information on juice fasts/cleanses go to www.avitality.co.il

Index

A

B

C

N

O

P

Q

R

S

T

U

V

W

Z

NOTES

禪

NOTES

禪

NOTES

禪

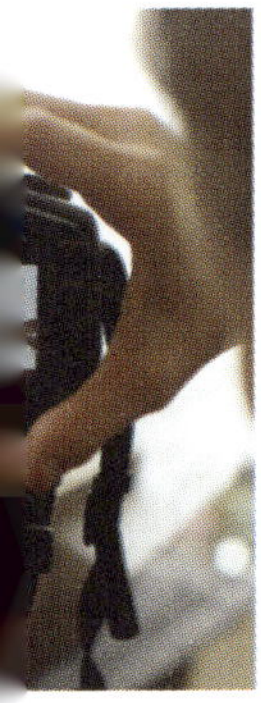

THANK YOU

多謝

To my beloved Family: My dear mother Simcha and my late father Gabi Sebbag, of Blessed Memory. To Doron & Adi Sebbag and the entire ORS family, my sister Dorit Gellerman-Sebbag. To my amazing sons Yossi, Mikey, Gabriel "Babi", Joy & Yonatan. To Yuli and Tati Hava. To my extended family aunts, uncles, cousins, nieces and nephews. To the entire Sebbag-Toledano-Zafrani families for my Moroccan roots and upbringing.

A big thank you to the amazing production crew, for your assistance throughout this journey, your trust and support. Thank you to the talented photographer Michal Lenart. Thanks to my wonderful friends Efrat Marciano (Mor) and Orit Rahmani, Tamar Mor-Sela, Ingrid Kutner, Elza Puin and Diane Ayoun, Cathrine Gerson for the index and Elizabeth Zauderer for the English translation.

To the Kwan um school of Zen: A special thanks to my dearest Zen teacher Yuval Gil and his remarkable mother Rowena, thanks to you I found my way.

Zen master Soeng Hyang, Zen Master Wu Bong in Memory, Zen Master Dae Jin in Memory, Zen Master Bon Shim, Jo Potter JDPSN, Zen Master Ji Kwang, Zen Master Dae Bong, To all the Sangha for allowing me to grant presents from my kitchen, cooking retreats and special occasions.

To my partner, Zohar Zemach Wilson on our joined voyage. Ruthi Roi-Weinstein (Taatzomot), Anat Tzahor (Yoga Dharma), Efrat Abramson, Ida Tzitzula, Revital and Shahar Lev Ari, Renana Lee-Horesh, Tammy Hahn, Lior Hikri, Dafna Botzer, Tamar Tzoberi, Shimi, Nomind, the Moa Oasis Family, Ayala Rish-Lakish, Zipi Pukka-Israel, Ori BioGreen, Niv Jammoka, Yossi Kefir - King Solomon Wisdom.

A special thank you to my dearest friends: Yahli Admati, Ruth Leshem, Roni Oren, Daphna and Danny Abraham, Amalia Lazrov, Jackie Waik, Bella Blum (RIP), Simcha Ziv (RIP), Gili Ben Ami (RIP), and Shosh Cviat (RIP). Shira Levy, Eran Barkan, Esty and Oren "the Important Man", Nava Siman Tov.

Thanks to all those who contributed products, kitchenware, clothing and accessories: Tema Design, Tamarindi, Hibino, Kneh Kash, Ayelet Guy Curtain Studio, Nook Atmosphere, Hercules Parquet, Daphna Butcher Pottery, Billy Chinese Pottery.

Special thanks to my talented friend Eddie Goldfine, for designing this book and for his friendship. And to all my friends, students and teachers along the way.